"DESIGN" IN A MANAGEMENT SENSE GOES BEYOND THE PHYSICAL ENVIRONMENT. IT'S ABOUT ORDERING RELATIONSHIPS THAT ENCOURAGE THE CREATIVITY AND COOPERATION THAT BENEFIT AN ORGANIZATION.

RICHARD SWETT

AN ENVIRONMENT IS TALKING ALL THE TIME—
AND A LOT OF THAT TALKING IS MUMBLING AND
GRUMBLING AND WHISPERED COMPLAINTS.

BRUCE MAU

MANY ORGANIZATIONS WANT TO CREATE
BETTER WORKPLACES. THE REASON THEY
FAIL IS THAT THEY DON'T KNOW HOW.

DANIEL PINK

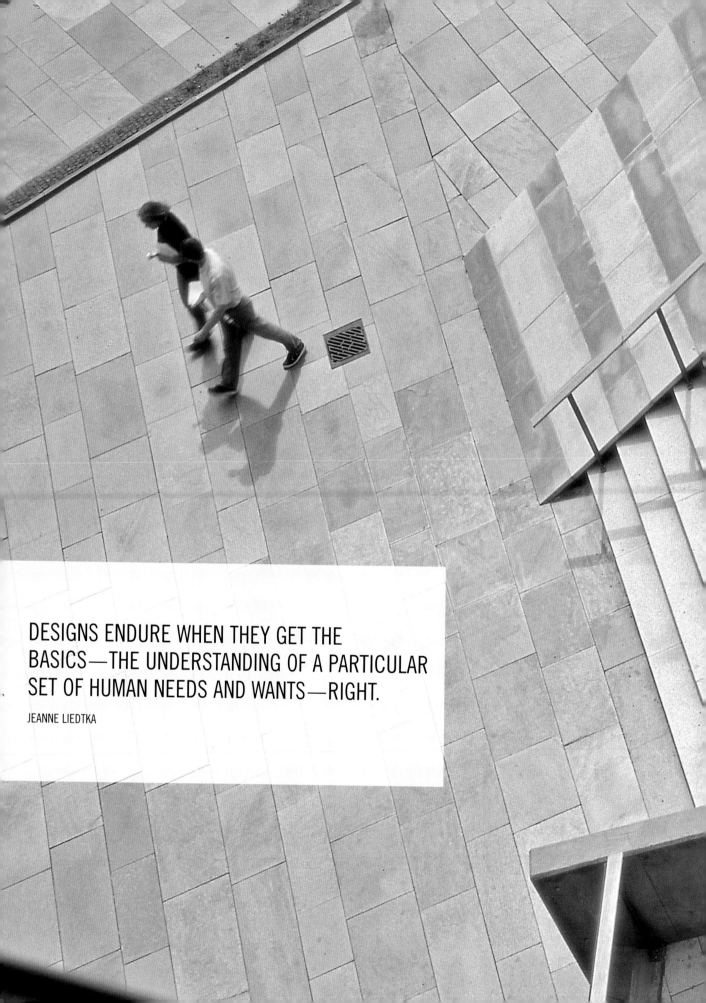

DESIGNS ENDURE WHEN THEY GET THE BASICS—THE UNDERSTANDING OF A PARTICULAR SET OF HUMAN NEEDS AND WANTS—RIGHT.

JEANNE LIEDTKA

THE OFFICE BUILDING IS THE ARK IN WHICH BUSINESS SAILS. GOOD MANAGERS UNDERSTAND THEY EXCEL IF THEIR BUILDING SUPPORTS THE WAY THEY WANT THEIR FIRM TO FUNCTION.

ALEXI MARMOT

THE OPPORTUNITY IS TO TAKE A BUILDING'S
MESSAGE AND TO MAKE IT A SONG, TO
MAKE IT SING ABOUT VALUE AND POTENTIAL
AND POSSIBILITIES.

BRUCE MAU

PHYSICAL STRUCTURES—WHETHER BODIES OR BUILDINGS—FUNCTION BEST WHEN WE PAY ATTENTION TO WHAT'S HAPPENING INSIDE.

ASTRID PUJARI

Östberg Library of Design Management

ISBN 978-0-9818989-5-7

Book Design: Ian Rapsey & Co. with StudioLAB

Printed in China

Published by: Greenway Communications, LLC, a division
of The Greenway Group, 25 Technology Parkway South,
Suite 101, Atlanta, GA 30092 1 800.726.8603

www.greenway.us

CHANGEDESIGN

Conversations about architecture as the ultimate business tool

nbbj

CONTENTS

INTRODUCTION

A discussion has been happening in the business and design worlds. While business magazines launched online design and innovation channels and business schools introduced design programs, designers have begun to emphasize performance as never before. In an environment compelled to recalibrate the engines of growth and prosperity, the discussion around design's critical role in business has focused on the value of innovation and design solutions.

When successful, design solutions forego predictable answers in favor of transformational results and collaborative partnerships. The best new buildings enable new ways of working that are critical in an environment of change. Whether it is at the scale of global systems or local markets, guiding missions or on-the-ground strategies, streamlining organizational structures or day-to-day operations, change happens in a place that supports it.

In 2006, architectural firm NBBJ launched an initiative called Change Design. It explores new directions, tools, and methodologies for developing environments that are performance driven, humanistic, and sustainable. The initial expression of that exploration, Change Design: Conversations about Architecture as the Ultimate Business Tool, presented the results of a series of conversations, workshops, brainstorming sessions, and panel discussions. It demonstrated how innovation, performance, collaboration, and transformation are engaging the business and design worlds in a conversation about the value of design in business. Now, this expanded edition of that original book updates the growing body of evidence for performance-based design with new conversations, essays, and a section devoted to Change Design Futures—an inside look at the next generation of projects to embrace the potential of Change Design in a changing world.

DESIGN
CHANGE
CONVERSATIONS

Fourteen visionary leaders of prominent corporations, educational organizations, healthcare enterprises, governmental entities, and research institutions share their insights on using design as a tool for cultural change. In their own words, the leaders, and the designers who worked with them, talk openly about the ambitions, risks, hurdles, and accomplishments of their "change design" projects.

NO PAPER, NO OFFICE, NO PROBLEM

Telenor CEO Jon Fredrik Baksaas transformed his public monopoly into a competitive multinational by canceling cubicles, losing land lines, and creating a collaborative workforce on the banks of a Norwegian fjord.

JON FREDRIK BAKSAAS
PRESIDENT AND CEO, TELENOR

Since 2002, Jon Fredrik Baksaas has been in charge of the day-to-day management of operations at Telenor ASA and in the Telenor Group. He joined Telenor in 1989 and was made Deputy CEO in 1997. Baksaas has held positions as Finance Director, Executive Vice President, and CEO of TBK AS, a subsidiary specializing in system integration. Before joining Telenor, Baksaas held finance-related positions in Aker AS, Stolt-Nielsen Seaway and Det Norske Veritas. He is a board member of Svenska Handelsbanken AB. Baksaas holds a Master of Science in Business Administration from the Norwegian School of Economics and Business Administration in Bergen and has additional qualifications from IMD in Lausanne, Switzerland.

Describe your own workspace at Telenor's new Fornebu headquarters. What does it look like? We made a point of standardizing all workstations, so as the CEO of Telenor I have the same type of workstation as all my colleagues. We have an open space area for about 15 people called the Group Management Area. This open area facilitates easy communication and information sharing between the different group managers. On the other side of the coin, we make sure we maintain a versatile area where we can concentrate and work in more silent modes.

Let's go back to when you first started to plan for this new headquarters. Telenor was at a turning point. Can you tell me how the company was changing? In the mid '90s the telecommunication industry in Europe was undergoing a lot of changes. Competition was the target in all markets, and liberalization was taking place at high speed. Several licenses—particularly in the mobile field—were issued for the national market, and Telenor had to prepare to move from a monopoly situation into a competitive situation. And we did that in two ways. We started to prepare ourselves for the new market conditions in Norway, and we started an international program where we took our competencies into other markets.

You could say that having been a monopoly operation for quite a number of years—we celebrated our 150th anniversary in 2005—getting competitors in the domestic market was quite a change. This moves the core competencies of the group—over a long period of time, of course—from being very technology-focused to becoming a more customer-oriented company. And this change was stimulated by also co-locating all our activities into a brand-new headquarters building.

You had 40 buildings scattered throughout Oslo? Yes, we had more than 40 different addresses around Oslo, approximately 250,000 square meters (2.7 million square feet) altogether. At that point in time, we also had a fair amount of leasing contracts, which made it easier for us to take the step of moving into a head-quarters, which we took responsibility for ourselves.

So, we were very deliberate in our co-location efforts in order to build a business culture around the co-location exercise, and in hindsight it has worked in a tremendous way.

Would you say the main role that a new building could play in meeting the challenges the company faced was in creating a new culture? Well, the different communication platforms lived in separate silos. The mobile guys lived in one building, the fixed guys lived in a second building, the TV guys lived in a third building, and from there you could go on.

And all these operations were, in a way, fully set up, independent companies, with their own reception, security measures, server platforms, and so on. We organized the co-location efforts in such a way that we could very easily spot and recognize double work functions; we made people visible to each other in a completely new fashion. And here comes the architecture and gives a helping hand in facilitating communication across business units in a very attentive way.

When you launched the competition to find designers for the building, you said—and you were very explicit about this—that your ambition was to create Scandinavia's leading workplace for innovative activities. What did you have in mind? We were of the opinion that the traditional way—at least, what we felt we had in our history—was that people were working in very closed environments, in closed groups. And as a manager, at that point in time, we had to spend a lot of energy getting one core competence to play with another core competence in another company. We were of the opinion that if we could let these groups meet each other, in a more easy physical atmosphere, it would generate new ideas, reduce time to market, and increase Telenor's ability to keep pace with the general market developments in the telecommunications area.

You had seven design firms on the competition short list. Of the schemes presented—why did you pick this one? The final concept that we decided to go for was called the Uffizi. The Uffizi is a palace, designed by an Italian architect back in the 16th century, I think. The team called it the Uffizi in the Wall, meaning that two buildings were, in a way, mirrored towards each other, creating a plaza in between them, and with this approach we could maintain separation between business areas. At the same time we could create an arena where people could meet easily, and there were very small distances from one unit to another.

I think we really achieved that, and if there is something that our employees are very satisfied with these days it is that it is easy to meet, it is easy to exchange views, it's done in an informal way, and the number of formal meetings has decreased quite significantly.

But it requires that we, from a management point of view, really put people together so that they increase their knowledge about each other, professional as well as personal.

7,500 EMPLOYEES 6,000 WORKSTATIONS

PROJECT PROFILE

Telenor is Norway's largest telecommunications provider, with 2.7 million mobile subscriptions and 2.3 million fixed phone lines and ISDN subscriptions. Outside Norway, Telenor serves more than 75 million mobile subscribers through its ownership stakes in 11 international mobile operators. Telenor also serves 2.7 million satellite and cable-based TV subscribers.

Telenor consolidated 40 buildings in the Oslo area into a new waterfront headquarters built on the main runway of Fornebu, the city's former international airport on the Oslo fjord.

Two crescent-shaped buildings house eight office wings, each with its own atrium. Employees are assigned to one of 200 work zones accommodating 40 people each.

At 137,000 square meters (1.5 million square feet) Telenor's new campus is the biggest corporate headquarters in the Nordic region. Despite its size, the new campus has reduced the amount of space the company occupies by 40 percent and cut its annual operating costs by $3 million.

The building is the world's largest implementation of "hot desking"—where employees do not have dedicated workspaces. The headquarters can cater to 7,500 employees sharing 6,000 workstations, 225 meeting rooms, 40 video conferencing sites, four restaurants, and three coffee bars.

The building has one of Europe's largest wireless local area networks, with 32,000 ports for phone and data exchange.

It is a paper-free environment. Mailrooms scan printed documents, send the electronic files to recipients, then shred and recycle the paper. Meeting room electronic whiteboards convert meeting notes to electronic files.

As a technology company you have an opportunity to be ahead of the technology curve. How did you believe that technology was going to change the way work was done, and how did your new building need to respond to the changes that you were anticipating? From a technology point of view, we in this building were the first ones in the Nordic countries to integrate mobile services and PC data connections in the same package. As an example, we made it so that all employees moved to mobile phones as their communication medium.

Are there any land lines? I'm talking to you on the land line in a meeting room today. We have land lines in our meeting rooms, but not at workstations.

Not at all? Practically not at all. Which means that nearly everyone has only one number, and you will not find me, for example, labeled in a directory in Norway with anything other than my mobile number.

    If I get a call that enters into my voice mail, I can retrieve that voice mail from my portable PC. This enables me to carry forward a voice mail message to my neighbor, if I so want, if it is of relevance for others to know of a discussion that has been taking place on the voice mail platform.

    And over time this becomes a new way of working, a new way of communicating efficiently with each other.

And how did you need to have the building support that new way of working with each other? The building is physically established with 220 security zones. We could basically have 220 competitors being looked after in this building without interfering with each other. But we are also able to allocate access between groups

WE CAN MOVE A THOUSAND PEOPLE FROM ONE SECTION TO ANOTHER SECTION OVER THE WEEKEND.

in our company in such a way that people can visit each other in a very easy manner. And we also created an environment—an atrium type of common area—where people could sit down, meet informally, and also be networked because it's a wireless access platform here as well. You will find groups of people, three to four persons, sitting in the atriums of this building in such a way that they have both a very nice, stimulating area to be in, as well as having the efficiency in place for that kind of communication.

Another key concept for the building was that there would be far fewer desks than there were people, because of the way this mobile technology liberates employees from their desks. In the 1990s, there were some famous failed experiments in this kind of corporate hot desking, like Chiat/Day in Los Angeles. What convinced you that it would work for Telenor in your new headquarters? I think this is an aspect which is very different from organization to organization. We have activity areas in Telenor that run one-to-one, desks and people, but then we have other environments that run one-to-one-point-five, which means that we are able, in particular in the marketing areas of our groups, to have more people than desks. This, of course, creates a new flexibility in how you operate your workforce.

You know that any big company has a core structure for people-moving. You order the carpenters, you order all the handicraft men to adjust the new areas, and then come the computer guys afterwards to do the adjustments. Whereas in this building, we don't have that kind of obstacle. We can move a thousand people from one section to another section over the weekend, because there is no reprogramming; the portable PC is active and has the same profile wherever you are in the building. The moving cost, under a reorganization effort, for example, is close to zero.

As superbly functional as it is now, I imagine this way of working could have been a rather frightening idea for some staff when you were in the planning stages. How did you deal with that? Well, it was. It was scary for the corporate management as well as for the employees. So we developed a three-dimensional virtual-reality computer model to let people come and visit the new working area long before the buildings were really there. It also enabled us to, in a very lively way, execute the final setting of what these offices were to look like, including the colors and the views into the Norwegian scenery, because we also integrated daylight and sunlight into the 3D rooms, so we could get well associated with it in advance.

Then, corporate management—with myself as the main motivation force—ran a program where we really stimulated and motivated the middle management to take this environment into their own hands and make their own working habits, coming out of the cell-like type of offices into the more open space areas that we have here. These are not big spaces. I think the maximum number of workstations we have in one open space area is between 30 and 40.

At the same time there are some big spaces in the building. This is a very large building, is it not? It is a large building. Initially [before the move] we had 250,000 square meters (2.7 million square feet) and we took that down to 137,000

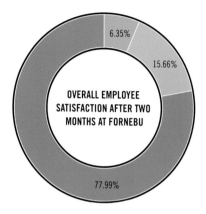

OVERALL EMPLOYEE SATISFACTION AFTER TWO MONTHS AT FORNEBU

6.35%
15.66%
77.99%

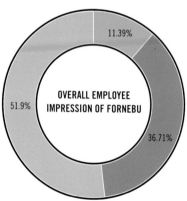

OVERALL EMPLOYEE IMPRESSION OF FORNEBU

11.39%
51.9%
36.71%

MORE POSITIVE

LESS POSITIVE

AS EXPECTED

(1.5 million), so we achieved quite a significant reduction in number of square meters. But this building is itself divided by eight entrances, and each is given a label—A, B, C, D. If I'm going to section number 7B I know that it's entrance B, seventh floor, so it's a very simple and unified structure to identify where I am in the building.

Once staff had actually moved in, how did they respond to this new environment, both in terms of locating themselves physically and also locating themselves as members of this company, this community? Here we really did so much preparatory work that the first group of employees who moved in here generated envy among those who hadn't moved in. Which means that when the next flow came, three months later, it all went smoothly.

You've done some surveys on how the staff feel about the new building. What did those show? We've run, on an annual basis, statistics on these kinds of questions. We have always received a high rating on how satisfied people feel about being here, and we have between four and five percent expressing a dissatisfaction with this kind of environment, which we probably would have anywhere.

So, the great majority are satisfied. They are satisfied, or they are even expressing that the environment here beats expectations. And this also has something to do with the exterior and where this building is placed, because it's located in one of the most magnificent areas, close to the Oslo fjord. So, from a scenic point of view it is a very beautiful site.

And the building is able to take advantage of that? The building plays on that. The building has been created in such a way, both by the selection of materials as well as from how windows are designed, to take advantage of the northern lighting, as well as the sunsets.

You've been in the building for several years now. How does it seem to be maturing, and how do you feel that Telenor is maturing with it? Well, we have to refresh ourselves on the original concept. We are also trying to get rid of some habits that we see and don't like. And as a CEO I urge all the working groups of this building to constantly debate and discuss the quality of work and how the environment functions.

And we see an interesting effect here: when we are hiring people from external sources, they are fascinated by this type of environment, and we can really use the building and the structure as a differentiating factor. But also, as newcomers, they have not lived through the process of maturing into a regular way of operating, and some of these people are asking, "Where can I get an office? Where can I lock myself in?" And then we have to repeat the basic philosophy of the whole system.

When you first planned the building, what were you hoping it would communicate to people both inside and outside the company about Telenor? And how do you feel it is functioning in that regard? We feel that when we have visitors here who have something to do with Telenor in one way or another, they express fascination and they also express that, "Wow, I didn't expect something like this." The person who expressed this most clearly was Hewlett-Packard's [former CEO] Carly Fiorina, who was here for the opening in September 2002. She hadn't expected to see such a powerful building expressing as much as it did to her on first impact, which was for us an interesting reaction to note. We've seen it with several others who have come here.

CHANGE DESIGN
TOOL IN ACTION

SIMPLIFY COMPLEXITY

To help clients use architectural design for change, NBBJ has developed a set of tools, including one that brings order to complex, even apparently chaotic settings by recognizing patterns and establishing systems. On the Telenor headquarters, NBBJ used a tool called "Simplify Complexity" to deliberately identify the basic collaborative structures within the large, multifaceted company, represent those structures with a concept about organizational scale, and apply the concept in the design of the headquarters.

SEE PAGE 182 FOR MORE INFORMATION ABOUT THIS TOOL.

POWERS OF TEN

Telenor said that, although they have 7,500 employees, their ultimate teams are groups of 40. But they also know that collaboration happens in groups of four. And you've got to think about the one individual person. So we said, "Okay. Let's talk about an architecture that embraces 40 people and their coffee bar, their community space, their bulletin board." Every group of 40 has its own place, and within it, places for one and four. There are 10 groups of 40 around an atrium with a café or a pool table.

The next order of magnitude is 400, but you can still visualize your context: I'm in Building Number Seven, and in it are a bunch of groups of 40. Each of those buildings of 400 latches onto embracing arms that are huge circulation paths and atriums. And those arms embrace the open gathering place in the plaza. So, walking into the building you go from being one to four to 40 to 400 to 4,000. The scale of the architecture matches the increases, so you never feel lost.

SCOTT WYATT, PARTNER, NBBJ

You have many visitors, do you not? Remember that the general public can walk the plaza. This is an open area, even though it's an industrial area, and on a day like this I can look out the window and see people enjoying the sunset on the beach of the Oslo fjord. We have created an after-hours environment that is attractive, both for employees as well as for people living in the neighborhood. And on a yearly basis, 5,000 visitors tour the building.

So your experiment here is proving to be one that has applications elsewhere. We hope so. And we also find that a lot of Telenor customers come here and find inspiration for how to rearrange their own working environment, using the combination of architecture, technology, and surroundings.

As you continue to develop new products and services, how will the building and its infrastructure accommodate them? There are constant changes in how our communication platform is delivering new functionality to its users, and we are developing those kinds of functionality enhancements at top speed.

And the building is able to accommodate those shifts? Absolutely. We have not yet encountered an obstacle in that sense. We have already upgraded the wireless access platform for PCs, because the wireless technology has developed tremendously over the last four years.

And that has been something that you've been able to accomplish without a lot of trouble and money? Of course, any migration is not free, but being a technology company, this is our profession, so when we're doing something like this, based on our needs, we reckon that there are customers out there who will be interested in the same functionality enhancements. That's how this market moves, and we've been able to meet that kind of development.

As part of your growth as an international company you've been looking at markets in central and eastern Europe and in Asia. What future does the Fornebu model have in those cultures? That's an interesting question. In 2005 we inaugurated a new office building in Kiev, in the Ukraine; we will open a new office building in Malaysia; and we are in the midst of establishing a new office building in Islamabad in Pakistan. All these buildings are taking elements from Fornebu, but they are not going as far as we have on the standardization of the workstations, because these are societies which are more hierarchical than Scandinavian societies. But from a technology point of view, with integration of mobile and PC services, we have more or less the same standards.

And we see that our local managers pick up the ideas here from our head office and use them back home when they make their decisions on how they want to sit, want to work, want to create working environments for the employees.

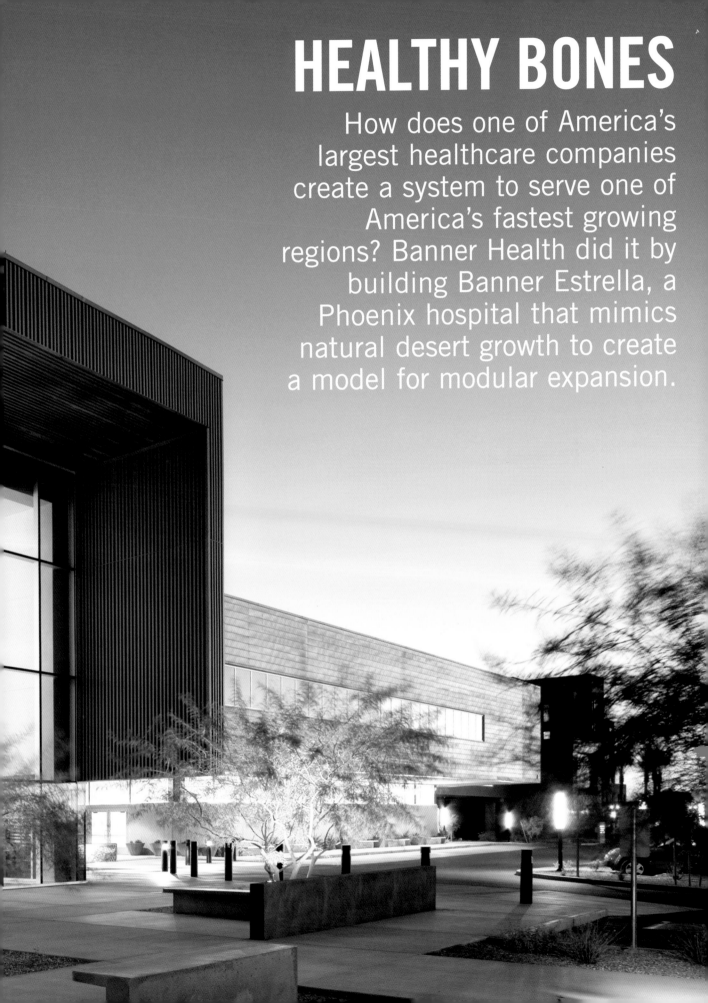

HEALTHY BONES

How does one of America's largest healthcare companies create a system to serve one of America's fastest growing regions? Banner Health did it by building Banner Estrella, a Phoenix hospital that mimics natural desert growth to create a model for modular expansion.

SUSAN S. DORIA
FORMER SENIOR VICE PRESIDENT, STRATEGIC DEVELOPMENT, BANNER HEALTH

At the time of the project, Susan Doria was responsible for business and organizational development across Banner Health, which was formed in 1999 through the merger of Samaritan Health System and Lutheran Health Systems. Doria oversaw the company-wide functions of Planning, Development and Construction, Learning and Communications, Brand Services, and Grants and Appropriations. Prior to this role, Doria, who joined Samaritan Health System in 1986, served in a series of staff and executive positions. She received both a Bachelor of Science degree and Master of Health Services Administration degree from Arizona State University. Doria devotes many hours of community work as a board member of HomeBase Youth Services, a non-profit agency helping homeless youth.

Phoenix, Arizona, is one of the fastest-growing cities in the United States. Can you tell me where that population boom is coming from and why it's happening? Phoenix has become the fifth-largest metropolitan area in the country. It has an attractive climate and a growing cultural, retail, and education base. Most of our migration comes from California, and the Midwest is a close second behind that. In the past decade, it has really boomed. We're reaching a critical mass now, where there are sophisticated activities along with interesting architecture for people who are quite cosmopolitan.

What did your research tell you about the healthcare needs of this incoming population? We've been looking to make a major investment in growth to keep up with the population boom, and we've started to think about the types of facilities we would design to accommodate this growth. First and foremost, it's about picking the right location, and second it's about adaptable design. We're having a hard time retrofitting and renovating many of our existing facilities to adapt to the changes in care delivery that we're seeing today and will continue to see into the future. We had to think about it relative to new technologies and how spaces and places would have to change to adapt to the technology. One thing we've found in all of our healthcare planning to date, going back a couple of decades, is that there wasn't enough forethought in terms of how to make space much more flexible as technology changes.

Before you started to build Banner Estrella in West Phoenix, what healthcare facilities did Banner have in the Phoenix area? We have eight hospitals in Arizona, seven in the metropolitan Phoenix area. We were already the major healthcare player in town, with upwards of a third of the market share. We saw an opportunity to go into an underserved area that had not been addressed from a hospital need perspective because hospitals' operating performance had been depressed for a while. Many of our competitors didn't have the financial wherewithal to invest in new facilities. When we had the ability to invest, we jumped on the opportunity to go into that new community and build a new campus for it.

Banner Estrella was built, for a hospital, extraordinarily fast—36 months from the time the design team started to the time the hospital actually opened. Why such an accelerated schedule? Being one of the first to market is important for our industry. We had new competitors coming into the area—there was one hospital that opened about a year before we did, so we didn't want to have too much lag time here. There was also a lot of demand for the Banner product from area community leaders and interest from physicians who wanted to expand their practices and preferred to do it with Banner.

What implications did a fast-track schedule like that have initially for the design? Getting clarity of the overall concept on the front end was a key driver. We thought of this as our franchise model for future campuses, because we knew that other market segments were also growing quickly. When we started design work we saw this as the launch of Banner's "Hospital for the Future." We weren't just designing the hospital that sits on this site, we were designing Banner's model for tomorrow's hospital. We had inclusive, multidisciplinary stakeholder involvement on the front end to explore what we needed to take into consideration. And frankly, because of all the problems we have with our current facilities, this concept became almost like marching orders for the design group. Address these problems and do not design like today's environment. Think about how care is changing, think about how clinicians and teams of people are interacting, think about what's important in the healing process. Get beyond any biases you have about healthcare and how it should be delivered today. Start with fresh eyes, from the patient perspective.

What are some of the problems that you're having today in the facilities that you're trying to retrofit? One of the biggest problems we face is that campuses weren't designed to accommodate growth over time, yet they always have to grow and add more beds as the population fills in. Unfortunately, your core chassis isn't flexible; you have hard-wall departments next to each other and there is no room to expand. So the facility doesn't flex for growth; it also doesn't flex for changes in technology, equipment that's getting smaller or equipment that's getting much larger. So it's really hard, if you didn't design the campus to flex with growth demands, to go back and retrofit it later.

Can you describe how the growth design that is built right into the new facility works? The concept is pretty simple. The building is organized along a central spine with all the special mechanical, electrical, and plumbing needed to create patient-safe spaces. If you don't plan from that kind of guts, it becomes very expensive to move these systems later on. The diagnostic and treatment components, which change over time as new modalities of care arise, are designed to be much more like medical office space. They're designed like a honeycomb. You start on a grid pattern with the smallest D&T area that you need, and then you build on that grid pattern as your growth goes. Patient care towers are also

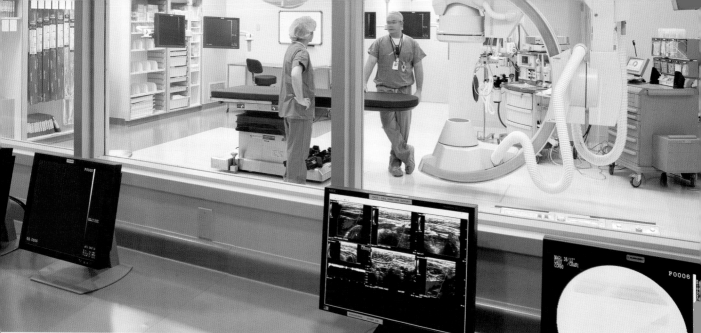

PROJECT PROFILE

Phoenix-based Banner Health is one of the largest, non-profit healthcare systems in the country, with 22 hospitals in seven western states: Alaska, Arizona, California, Colorado, Nebraska, Nevada, and Wyoming.

Banner Estrella is the first ground-up hospital to come online as part of Banner Health's development program in this region.

According to 2002 U.S. Census data, the Southwest is the fastest-growing region in the United States, and the suburbs of Phoenix are among the nation's fastest growing communities.

Located on 50 acres in West Phoenix, the new hospital includes a full-service,167-bed acute care tower, medical office buildings, and an outpatient surgery center.

The medical campus provides surgery, cancer care, cardiac services, emergency services, and a comprehensive women and infants program. It is currently able to handle 4,000 births per year.

A new caregiving model breaks down the traditional clinical silos. Here, surgery, cardiac, and imaging services share a single clean core.

The hospital is designed for systematic growth: it can accommodate a 10- to 20- year growth plan by adding two additional towers, for a total of 600 beds.

Information technology has eliminated the traditional nurses' station. Instead of a central nurses' hub, the hospital's clinical integration suite includes all the acute care and critical care nursing functions.

modular. Each tower can hold almost 200 beds. We can add towers, without disrupting the first one or any of the central spine.

Has this become the model that you were referring to earlier? Yes. It's a brilliant design in the way that you can grow something over time without disrupting current operations. And that's the problem: how do you ever close down a hospital to do a major construction project? From a patient care perspective, where would those patients go? And think of all the revenue you'd lose during that year of construction.

And this allows you to respond to the market need. Right, exactly.

So the term that you referred to earlier, Hospital for the Future, for Banner literally meant what? We had eight components that made our Hospital for the Future. One of the first is flexible and adaptable design; that's the whole piece that I've been talking about. Another major component involves creating a healing environment. There's been a lot of research done about music, light, color, texture, smell, how you use space and bring the outdoors in and so forth, that has really impacted the design of healthcare facilities so it can contribute to better patient care outcomes.

How do those theories actually get incorporated into the building itself? Lighting, just as an example, is very important, so the patient rooms are designed with access to windows and lots of sunlight. Another component is patient-centered care. The rooms are designed to accommodate family members who spend the night, because the family is now involved in the caregiving process and has become much more like a patient advocate. You have to be very clever about how you design different zones of care—including sterile environments for the clinician—so that there's maximum efficiency of the space, and a lot more efficiency of staff time, too. We were also looking at how to improve patient care outcomes, so we have designed what are called acuity-adaptable rooms. In many hospitals, patients start off in the ICU after very intensive surgery, go to a step-down unit and then to a regular medical surgical bed before they go home. In the course of those hand-offs they're with different caregivers and may be on different floors. Orders, directions, care become fragmented. There's room for human error. In the acuity adaptable model, we have a core of rooms on each floor that go up and down in intensity of care and the patient doesn't have to move anywhere.

Another aspect of the Hospital for the Future is something called "paper light," which is not quite the same as paperless, but is heading in that direction. Estrella is the first place that Banner has installed a completely electronic environment, where nearly all documentation is done electronically. We have stations both in and outside of the room where clinicians can pull up records and make notes electronically. We watched videos of what usually happens on nursing floors and saw how much time the nurse or physician spends walking around looking for the patient chart. It adds to time delays and information isn't always collected appropriately in the patient chart. Making this electronic is not only very efficient, it also improves quality of care, because you can build in systems that actually have rules to check things that have been ordered. With everything electronic, there are many new tools that can enhance the clinician's ability to deliver better quality care.

How much have these tools been applied, to your knowledge, in other hospital settings? Not a whole lot yet. It's a very expensive investment, and there's a lot of push-back from people in the system because it changes the way things are

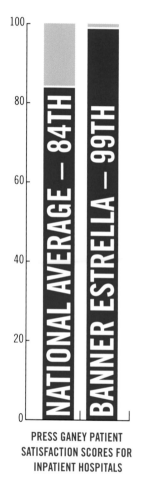

PRESS GANEY PATIENT
SATISFACTION SCORES FOR
INPATIENT HOSPITALS

Source: 2004 National Inpatient Priority Index, Press Ganey. Reflects average mean score; survey of over 2 million patients treated at over 1,500 U.S. hospitals.

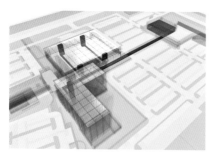

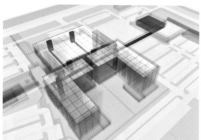

IT'S A BRILLIANT DESIGN IN THE WAY THAT YOU CAN GROW SOMETHING OVER TIME WITHOUT DISRUPTING CURRENT OPERATIONS.

done. You have to invest time in redesigning your care processes. So, we were really excited to have the opportunity to install this from top to bottom in a whole new facility, where both the staff and the doctors who were recruited to the facility knew that this was the expectation.

And the care and the efficiency benefits—are they showing up demonstrably yet? We've been open about seven months, so it is too early to measure. Now, from a care satisfaction perspective we're hitting the mark. We do patient satisfaction surveys and benchmark ourselves. They're done by a third party and we're measured against other peer organizations around the country. Estrella's hitting the 99th percentile in patient satisfaction. For the rest of Banner's hospitals, in aggregate, we're trying to get to the top quartile, which is the 75th percentile. As a system, some of our hospitals are in the 40th percentile and we're trying to move them up to the 75th. Estrella's already hitting the top, because the facility is wonderful, the care experience is wonderful, people have new tools to provide better care.

There's another kind of amenity that Estrella offers, which is a bit harder to quantify: the building itself is designed to be a meditative, contemplative place. How did that concept evolve? When we thought about healthcare for the future, we didn't think of it just as an episodic, single event that impacts just one part of the body. We thought about the fact that it is an experience, and that experiences really do transform people. Then we said, "How can the space allow someone an opportunity to go more inside themselves, peacefully, to think about what the impact of that transformation is?" So, a lot of control is built into the mechanics of the patient care experience so that you aren't feeling like things are being done to you. You're the leader in this experience and you can go as deep as you want into your own transformation or not. The space is designed to be quiet and reflective.

HOSPITAL FOR THE FUTURE:
AUTOGENESIS

Few industries encounter as much continuous change as the healthcare industry and yet their facilities have typically been optimized for first use, rather than future use. The Hospital for the Future is designed to adapt to unknown futures, such as the inevitable shifts in patient care and emerging technologies. A new framework for design organizes the building into permanent zones for integrated circulation and infrastructure, and temporal zones for rapid change with minimized disruption and cost.

What kind of feedback have you been getting from staff since the opening? We're very lucky because we planned well, I would say, to select people who were going to feel comfortable in this kind of an environment and who were going to help us successfully take the physical structure into reality. Because it's one thing to design a building and then it's another to operate it the way that you envisioned. And so we had a selection and hiring process and an on-boarding process through orientation that was very deliberate, very specific. We actually had people audition for their jobs; we had them role play. At a new facility you often will get five applicants for every one new opening and, because of this, we had the ability to be very selective about the people we hired. We were very clear about the kind of environment we were hoping to create, what the design of the facility was supposed to contribute to, and what the role of the associate—we don't even call them employees—was at Estrella. It's one thing to create a new stage, but if you're doing the same old play you've missed the whole opportunity. I think we've done a good job. A start-up is always challenging, and we've had some adjustments

CHANGE DESIGN
TOOL IN ACTION

SITE SEE

In order to tie form to performance, architectural designers must be explicit about the tools they develop and use. One tool NBBJ has developed, "Site See," is used to provoke visionary thinking by looking beyond the immediate boundaries of the organization. For Banner Health's Estrella project, NBBJ used the tool to make critical observations about the unique physical and experiential characteristics of the hospital's natural setting, the Sonoran desert, observations that transformed the design into a special place with a unique healing environment.

SEE PAGE 184 FOR MORE INFORMATION ABOUT THIS TOOL.

DESERT MEDITATION

The design team was coming from the Pacific Northwest. If you go into the forest you can find five, seven, eight layers of life from the forest floor to the canopy—it's life crowding in upon life. What better source of inspiration for the team than the desert they found themselves in because the desert is singular in a very different way. There, you might find a plant with a 10-foot radius around it before you find the next plant. The desert is strong and severe but it also focuses the attention; there was so much to learn from it about making a meditative space.

The design concept started with observations about the desert floor—vast, flat, weathered land that's punctuated positively by mesas and negatively by canyons. And as soon as there's an event in the landscape, either positive or negative or both, life emerges—especially in places where you find water, like the canyons. When you add the desert sun to those events, the landscape becomes a huge clock, clearly expressing the passage of time.

The building was conceived of as one of those additive desert intersections coming up out of the ground with subtractive elements, like the exterior garden space enclosed between significant parts of the building. It was conceived as a place of contemplation. A place to focus on the significant events that occur throughout one's life.

CHRISTIAN CARLSON, PRINCIPAL, NBBJ

WE'RE A HOSPITAL FOR THE FUTURE. THAT WAS OUR GUIDING STAR. "ESTRELLA" MEANS "STAR" IN SPANISH. WITH THAT TO GO BACK TO, IT WAS EASY TO MAKE DECISIONS.

along the way, but we did a lot of work on what the associate experience was going to be like and how it was going to be different than any other employee experience in any of our other hospitals. For the most part, I think folks have been feeling that the experience that we described to them, that we hoped they would help us deliver for the patient, is also working for them.

It's extraordinary that all that was accomplished in 36 months. You designed the future! If you start out with the future in mind, and get everybody there first, the to-dos are pretty easy. Nobody's fighting. You always go back to your touchstone: "We're a Hospital for the Future." That was our guiding star. "Estrella" means "star" in Spanish. With that guiding star to go back to, it was easy to make decisions about which way to go, because the vision was really clear.

Since you created Estrella as a franchise model, are there things that you'll be changing in the next facility, having had the experience of building the first one? It's important to make sure that the facility reflects the market that you're going into and the demographic you'll be serving. That impacts where it's located, how it all fits into that environment, and the mix of services that you'll provide. We have been able to take the essence of the design and site-adapt it. For example, Estrella is a high-tech facility and more contemplative because of the intensity of care while the next facility we're doing, Banner Gateway, is more of a general community hospital. It won't, for example, have open-heart surgery capability or high-intensity cardiac services there; it's going to have more obstetrics and pediatrics. So it will have a less contemplative feel and more of a sense of community. There will be more of a sense of energy and vitality. And yet the overall concept of a flexible, adaptable healing environment, centered around the patient, will still be there. It will just morph slightly to accommodate the different activity going on. We're on a 30-month schedule for Gateway, so we've shaved off six months because we started with this franchise model. Now we're taking it out to our third project, which is actually going to start not as a hospital but as an ambulatory outpatient center and will grow into a hospital. So design, in terms of how you design to accommodate all that, has been very important.

BANNER GATEWAY MEDICAL CENTER

Banner Health rolled out the first "franchise" of its prototype Hospital for the Future with Banner Gateway Medical Center, a "well-care" hospital focused on outpatient and birthing services. As the NBBJ design team explains, this time the design challenge was adapting the acute-care prototype of Banner Estrella to a different facility type, patient population, regional influence, and community growth pattern.

At the heart of Banner's franchise concept is the ability to design for change and growth while interpreting design standards for better patient outcomes, safety, and patient satisfaction. The model is all about flow—the logistical movement of staff, patients, and materials necessary to sustain 24/7 hospital services. The "plug and play" aspect of the design—all mechanical systems are embedded along two edges of the diagnostic block—is critical, because it will allow the hospital to triple in size as needed. This long-term expansion strategy suits the needs of the hospital's location: Gilbert, Arizona, which has a rapidly growing population. By adapting the franchise model established with Banner Estrella, we were able to deliver the new hospital in 28 months, eight months faster than its prototype.

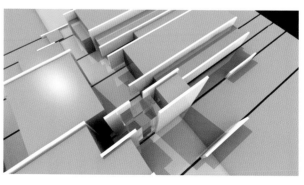

As with Estrella, the Arizona desert was an important source for Gateway's healing design. We studied the desert's canyons, and that led to striating the walls of the hospital like canyon rock. We were inspired by a canyon waterfall to run a water theme through the entire hospital. We represented the waterfall with a six-story glass wall at the entry, and stretched a variety of garden spaces—including a staff-only garden deck—along the central spine, or canyon, to provide respite for patients, staff and families.

MACKENZIE SKENE, PARTNER, NBBJ

A BREATH OF FRESH AIR

Vulcan Real Estate and the City of Seattle infuse new life into an old neighborhood by adapting a historic laundry building and a dark alley into a vibrant, sustainable, and pedestrian-oriented urban center.

ADA HEALEY
VICE PRESIDENT OF VULCAN REAL ESTATE

Vulcan's real estate strategies across the U.S. Pacific Northwest are under the direction of Ada Healey. She manages Vulcan's $1.8 billion in real estate assets, including approximately 2.5 million square feet (232,000 square meters) currently under construction or planned for delivery through 2011. Healey has been instrumental in the redevelopment of Seattle's South Lake Union neighborhood. She is an active participant in the Urban Land Institute, Downtown Seattle Association, Lake Union Park Corporate Committee and Build the Streetcar Campaign. Prior to joining Vulcan in 2001, Healey was Portfolio Manager at Clarion Partners, and served in various capacities in the company's acquisitions and asset management divisions. She holds an undergraduate degree from Duke University, and an MBA from New York University's Stern School of Business.

For people who aren't familiar with Seattle, can you describe the South Lake Union neighborhood and what it was originally? South Lake Union is in the geographic center of the city, located on one of Seattle's in-city waterways, Lake Union. It's a neighborhood that's about a hundred years old, and its original underpinnings were light industrial and manufacturing. It has always been on the forefront of innovation: Boeing built some of its early sea planes right there on the lake. There was a Ford Model T factory there, and a number of lumber yards and saw mills. Most of these original uses have relocated, and the neighborhood is now becoming a center of life sciences research, which is a 21st century industry.

What are some of the new enterprises that have been established in South Lake Union? The Fred Hutchison Cancer Research Center, which is one of the world's leading cancer research centers, is based in South Lake Union. The University of Washington School of Medicine, the number-one recipient of the National Institutes of Health funding for a public university, is expanding its research efforts in South Lake Union. A nonprofit called Seattle Biomedical Research Institute, which is leading research in AIDS and malaria, is also based there.

It's a community of early adopters. The people who have come to South Lake Union tend to be in the forefront of their industries. They tend to be on the cutting edge of what's next, because it takes a bit of a visionary to go into a

49%

LESS ENERGY
CONSUMED THAN TYPICAL
MULTI-TENANT OFFICE
BUILDINGS WITHIN FIRST
YEAR OF OCCUPANCY

neighborhood that's evolving. Microsoft has taken a lot of space in South Lake Union. Whole Foods is on the retail side, along with REI, the outdoor recreation supplier. One of the city's premier newspapers, the *Seattle Times*, is there. South Lake Union has been successful in attracting a demographic known as the creative class.

There's been a fair amount of discussion in recent years about how the creative class tends to be a marker for economic growth in cities. Yes, Richard Florida is quite famous for talking about this, and he considers Seattle one of the top 10 creative cities in the U.S. The creative class makes a living by relying on intellectual capital. This covers a wide range of people and organizations, but if you think about the companies doing research, those involved in media, and firms that are known for their creativity, these are the groups we are targeting. We're receptive to a very broad base of users, and the product we're designing responds to a lot of different organizations, but our primary target users are more open to change, they tend to see around corners and are open to new ideas and new ways of doing things. We want to take advantage of the inherent users in the South Lake Union market, and deliver a product that works for them.

Why is South Lake Union such a hot spot right now for the creative class, and for developers? It's a hot spot because there are multiple parcels available for development. Seattle is a city constrained by its natural boundaries. We have water everywhere, we have a lot of changes in geography, and the development capacity of the community is limited by some of those natural boundaries. South Lake Union is largely flat, and it's perfectly situated for re-development. It is very close to the central business district and shopping area, and it's also very close to a number of our arts and entertainment venues, so it affords both tenants and residents easy access to a lot of amenities, without having to live downtown.

There is a new 12-acre park going in at the base of the lake, Lake Union Park, and it's going to be a wonderful amenity for the community. It has a $30 million budget—the city and local governments have contributed $10 million, the Seattle Parks Foundation raised $10 million, and Vulcan made a contribution of $10 million. It's a great example of a public-private partnership. Phase Two should be completed in 2009. In the Cascade neighborhood of South Lake Union, we have Cascade Park, which was also renovated recently through a public-private partnership to make it more accessible to the neighborhood kids and more user-friendly to the people who live and work in the Cascade neighborhood. Other amenities include the new Seattle streetcar, which will serve as a connector to the region's major transit hub downtown.

So the time is now to revitalize this neighborhood. Vulcan owns 60 acres of property in South Lake Union, and we are re-developing that real estate into a mix of different uses. We're looking at developing between 40 and 45 percent of it as commercial or life sciences space; between 40 to 45 percent of it would be residential, both for rent and for sale, with the balance being retail and hospitality. Our goal is to develop that property as quickly as the market will support us. We have completed about 1.8 million square feet, and by the end of 2011, we will have completed about five million square feet.

You said your goal is to develop your property in South Lake Union quickly, but presumably you have to do that in accordance with Vulcan's real estate model, which is guided by a triple-bottom-line philosophy. Absolutely. A triple-bottom-line performance criteria is one of the goals that we instituted when we really began our development efforts in earnest, and I think it sets us apart from a number of our competitors in the market. We need to deliver returns back to the

organization using three criteria. The first is financial. We're on the for-profit side of Vulcan Inc., and we need to deliver market returns back to our owner so that we can continue to pursue projects. The second piece of the triple bottom line is that we want to have a positive impact on the community. We're very active in terms of outreach and want to make sure we deliver product to the market that's Class A, that the community is really excited about over an enduring period of time. And the third piece of the triple bottom line is being respectful of the environment, so we're focusing our efforts in the urban core and we're incorporating LEED and sustainable features into all of our projects. Sustainability and making excellent use of our natural resources is a huge priority for the organization, and for the real estate group in particular.

How has that triple bottom line guided the development of your cornerstone mixed-use project in South Lake Union, Alley24? The triple bottom line is woven through all of our development efforts, but Alley24 is a great example of it. We made a financial investment to deliver that project and we have delivered a market return back to our owners. In terms of community, the Cascade neighborhood, where Alley24 is located, is very interested in all of the development activity in their neighborhood, which is great, and we really embraced that. We had a number of neighborhood outreach meetings to engage the neighbors in conversation and discussion and I think we were able to design a much better project based on the feedback we got from the neighborhood stakeholders.

And for the third piece of the triple bottom line, Alley24 is incredibly sustainable. Part of it is an adaptive reuse of an existing building. Alley24 used to be the Richmond Laundry Building. The name Alley24 was derived from two

PROJECT PROFILE

Vulcan Real Estate is a division of Vulcan Inc.—Microsoft cofounder Paul G. Allen's company—and is responsible for the company's real estate strategies and investment portfolio.

Vulcan's plan for developing more than 10 million square feet (930,000 square meters) in South Lake Union is one of the U.S.'s largest urban redevelopment projects.

Occupying a full city-block, Alley24 integrates 180,000 square feet (16,700 square meters) of office space, 28,000 square feet (2,600 square meters) of retail, 4,400 square feet (400 square meters) of landscaped gardens and 172 residential apartments. It is one of the U.S.'s first LEED-certified mixed-use projects.

Ninety percent of the first residential tower was leased within three months of opening and currently 95 percent of all residential units are occupied. The retail space was 100 percent leased within two years and the fully-leased office space brought over 1,000 employees to the area.

The project participates in Seattle's Multi-Family Tax Exemption Program, making 20 percent of the residential units available at or below 60 percent of area median income.

Some corporate office workers are reporting a 30% decrease in sick days.

The commercial portion received LEED Silver certification for its Core and Shell; two office tenants achieved LEED Gold certification for corporate interiors; and the residential portion is tracking to LEED. South Lake Union is also part of the LEED for Neighborhood Development pilot program, with Alley24 as its anchor.

THE BUILDING INCORPORATES A LOT OF NATURAL DAYLIGHT, WHICH BOOSTS EMPLOYEE PRODUCTIVITY.

elements. The "alley" part references both the north-south alley on the site as well as the east-west alley that we incorporated into the project to allow for a cross-block connection. The "24" has a couple of meanings: It's a 24/7 facility because there are people working in the east building during the day and people living in the west building at night. The other part of the "24" comes from the fact that the women who worked in the laundry were Local 24 of the laundry union. In naming the project we wanted to recognize the rich history of the building and the women who had worked there many, many years ago. We actually saved a good portion of a historic structure and incorporated that into the residential part of the project.

We also constructed a new, 21st-century office building that includes a number of features that are unique in the local market as well as in the United States, in fact. The office side of Alley24 includes operable windows. It includes under-floor heating, ventilation, and air conditioning, which is very unusual in traditional office buildings, and because the floor is concrete on a podium, it's much more substantial than a traditional raised floor. Instead of hot and cold air blowing down from the ceiling, it comes up through diffusers in the floor, and people can move those vents, or they can close them if they're too hot or too cold. The building also has fixed sunscreens as well as motorized sun shades, so that we can balance the light and heat loads in the building to better control our heating and cooling. And when the temperature is appropriate, we can actually shut off the mechanical air and use the outside air—lots of studies have documented dramatic productivity increases by having access to fresh air. The building also incorporates a lot of natural daylight, which tends to boost employee productivity. What a novel concept, taking us back 200 years to properly light and ventilate our work space!

Many buildings these days claim to be green. What do you think makes the difference between claiming to be green and truly being green? Well, the U.S. Green Building Council puts out criteria that you must meet to be a green building, and the more features that you adopt as you design your building the greener you make it, whether that's with features that use water in a more thoughtful way—plants that don't require a lot of irrigation, dual-flush toilets—whether there's a green roof, a super-efficient HVAC system, more natural light so you don't need to turn on the light switch, whether you recycle on-site, whether you're close to public transportation. Every user has a different threshold and desire for being green, so there are degrees of green and degrees of additional expense. We have assumed a certain amount of risk. We've done a pretty good job of mitigating that risk, but to be a leader and to break the mold, you have to be willing to take a little bit more risk than the average developer or you won't do anything different.

On the flip side, what are the potential benefits for office tenants? The benefits come from lowering your operating expenses, because you're not using as much water, or as much energy to power your HVAC system. If you've got more natural light and fresh air, your employees are going to be more productive. You're hopefully going to do a better job of retaining your employees because they're going to feel they're in a healthy workspace and they're not going to get sick as much, and hopefully you're going to do a better job of recruiting new folks because it's a great place to work.

41 PERCENT OF COMMERCIAL TENANTS USE A MEANS OF TRANSPORTATION OTHER THAN SINGLE OCCUPANCY VEHICLES

88%

OF THE BUILDING IS LIT BY
NATURAL DAYLIGHT

90%

OF THE BUILDING IS HEATED
AND COOLED THROUGH OPERABLE
WINDOWS

How do the benefits work on the residential side? That has to do more with whether you're able to save on, say, your water expenses. You don't normally measure productivity in your home, you measure how much cost you're saving. And there are lifestyle benefits, and the knowledge that you're doing the right thing, because our natural resources are limited, and if we want to make sure there are resources for our children and grandchildren and so on, we need to be thoughtful about how we use them today.

You spoke earlier about involving neighborhood stakeholders to make a better project—how did your tenants contribute to your vision for Alley24? Having the architect serve in a dual capacity as both architect and tenant really challenged us, as developers, to come up with creative solutions that met the tenants' goals in terms of the program, that met the architects' goals in terms of aesthetics, and our goals in terms of project cost. Having everybody at the table arm-wrestling through some of those tough issues resulted in a much better project because we all had to actively engage so we understood each other's perspectives.

At the beginning of the project, the program for Alley24 wasn't completely defined, and the team spent a period of time exploring some of the key ideas of a sustainable building and a mixed-use one. What did you discover in that exploration? We discovered that you've got to run down a lot of rabbit holes before you get it right, and that's the process. We learned a lot from looking at different concepts before we settled on where we are today, which is a great place to be. When you think about progressive buildings, buildings that don't use as much energy, buildings that really support employee productivity, retention, and recruitment, you've got to think a bit out of the box. Since you can't buy those ideas off the shelf, you've got to throw a few things against the wall and talk about them and see what sticks. I would certainly say there are still more skeptics out there, waiting to see the "proof," than there are converts, but we're making progress.

Lyle Bicknell's specific areas of expertise as Senior Urban Designer with the City of Seattle's Department of Planning and Development include street and open space design, and creating successful, walkable communities. Before joining the City of Seattle, Lyle worked in the private sector as an architect and urban designer. He received his architecture degree from the University of Washington College of Architecture and Urban Planning.

LYLE BICKNELL
SENIOR URBAN DESIGNER, CITY OF SEATTLE DEPARTMENT OF PLANNING AND DEVELOPMENT

What elements would you consider make up a successful neighborhood?
From my perspective, success is when you have an active, alive neighborhood that meets the needs of not just one set of workers or one set of residents, but a range of people. It means sidewalks that are wide, streets that aren't too wide, traffic that is slow. It also means a mix of interesting destinations. I always like to think about "The City of the Short Distance." A city is successful when you only have to go a short distance to get what you need, whether it's a café or a restaurant or, in the case of South Lake Union, the streetcar—or maybe a sea plane to fly off to another destination!

Given those criteria, what is the city of Seattle's approach to development in the Cascade neighborhood of South Lake Union? The Cascade neighborhood is a really interesting place. It's been an intact neighborhood since the turn of the last century, and that's part of what makes it such a success. It had an early sawmill, it was the founding area for PACCAR trucks. It has also had a rich residential community. It had a large Russian community, and that's evidenced by Saint Spiridon Church, which is still here today. So the stage was set, but the question was: How do we make it even better? Certainly, sustainable, energy efficient buildings that are responsible and respectful of the environment—that's a big part of it. And making sure that we continue to have the same healthy mix of residential and commercial as we enter the 21st century.

You have seen the neighborhood go from what it was in the 90s to what it is now. How has Alley24 fitted into that transition? Well, this is one of the fastest changing neighborhoods in the city. Look around: you see all the construction cranes. That can be a difficult transition, especially for folks who have been here a long time. We're looking at 10,000 more residents in this neighborhood over the next 20 years. We need to have that happen gracefully and in a way that keeps the neighborhood livable as well as respecting all the good things that are already here. It really was a challenge to build something like Alley24. We have a lot of communities that are LEED residential and a lot of communities that are sustainably commercial, but to have that mixture in one place—it's really never been done before in quite this way in a neighborhood that has a strong identity and existing fabric. How do you insert something like this into a neighborhood in a way that complements it without compromising it?

How did you tackle that challenge? NBBJ did a lot of successful outreach. We had a number of visioning sessions where we would sit down over sandwiches and ask: What do we want this place to be? We would sit down with the design team, with neighbors, both existing neighbors and potential new neighbors, and get out our felt pens and begin to literally draw a vision for the new neighborhood. Sustainability was a big part of the neighborhood's concern; respecting the built heritage this neighborhood has; being a good neighbor, a good fit, those were all critical elements for what people wanted to see here.

What were the city's major concerns? A lot of folks, especially in our transportation department, were skeptical about the alley, and even I had some reservations. I was concerned that the alley might be too dark or not be a particularly vital place, but I trusted the design team and so I worked hard with our folks in the transportation department to convince them that an alley could be more

CHANGE DESIGN
TOOL IN ACTION

EXPLORE THE EXPERIENCE

Performance-based, rather than form-based, design meets the needs of the client, and the client's client. One powerful tool NBBJ uses to help discover those needs is called "Explore the Experience." It calls for really getting to know a client's needs by using ethnographic tools to study and live out their experiences. This tool took on a new meaning as the design team needed to investigate their own experiences when they decided to move their Seattle office to Alley24. As architect, interior designer, and tenant, NBBJ not only had to find the right questions to ask but had to study themselves to find the answers.

SEE PAGE 196 FOR MORE
INFORMATION ABOUT THIS TOOL.

SELF PORTRAIT

Setting out to design a new workspace for 400 designers was no easy task, especially because we would have to live with the outcome on a daily basis. And we were moving from a location that many employees had called home for more than two decades. So it was really important we got it right.

To understand our own workforce better, the design team conducted an extensive, in-house discovery process that involved the entire office. One of the exercises we conducted was a "day-in-the-life" study, where we had people record their thoughts, actions, and feelings throughout the day. We observed how people worked, where they interacted, and what the major distractions and obstacles were that they faced. Patterns of activity started to emerge, and we coupled our observations with how people felt and what they were thinking as their day unfolded so we were able to identify some common themes.

One of the major findings, not just from this particular activity but from our entire discovery process, was that people really valued the ability to connect and collaborate. The "day-in-the-life" exercise highlighted the challenges we

faced in our current environment to do so. Our studios were divided across six small and inefficient floor plates, which made it difficult for people to connect without having to travel between multiple floors. Our conference rooms were out of sight and closed off, and our common areas were tucked away from major circulation routes, which made us less likely to use them.

We wanted to minimize these inefficiencies in our new office and create areas that would become part of people's daily routines. In our new space, rather than having six, small

floors, we are spread across two, very large floors. So to make sure we got the connectivity we were looking for, we designed our workspaces around a central hub that runs through both levels. Functions like the library and model shop, which used to be hidden away, are brought into the hub. We've put big tables for impromptu meetings and open, informal critique areas right next to our kitchen and coffee bars, and we've opened up our conference rooms with glass walls and put them near these activity areas. The intent is for people to see, hear, and participate

in the social and creative dialogue that happens here. We've also organized our workstations around these hubs, so to get from one studio to another you don't have to hop on an elevator, you just walk through these areas of activity to get there.

ALAN YOUNG, PRINCIPAL, NBBJ

COMPOST
32.5 TONS
PER YEAR

GREEN INITIATIVE:

Tenants have been inspired to start up strategies to
"green" their office's internal workings. All commercial
and corporate tenants have implemented office-wide
composting programs, yielding approximately 32.5 tons
of compost a year with a portion of the compost being
used as fertilizer in the neighborhood park.

than just the typical place to pick up the garbage. It really could be an interesting
and healthy component of the city. Well, this project does great things with the
alley. It activates the alley and uses it in a way no other project in this city does.
I was just out looking at it a few minutes ago, and it's working. There are some
kids playing. It's a great place for strolling, it feels very comfortable and light. It
took some convincing, but in the end it paid off.

How does Alley24 fit in with the city's overall design for urban sustainability?
It's compact, complete, and connected. That's what we're interested in. It benefits
all the initiatives that we're looking at. We want to give examples of how high
density can be a great thing for people, but also meet our climate change concerns, too, because this kind of mixed-use, dense development is inherently
sustainable and, in terms of a carbon footprint, much better for the planet. In
a time when people can live anywhere they want—if you have skills, you can live
anywhere in the world—people are looking for places that are real, communities
that are genuine. And I think that's what you can find here.

IN PLANE VIEW

Boeing's Carolyn Corvi transformed an earthquake into a window of opportunity, building a factory-office hybrid where engineers, mechanics, support personnel and the program leadership share a workplace and a common outlook.

CAROLYN CORVI

FORMER VICE PRESIDENT—GENERAL MANAGER, AIRPLANE PRODUCTION,
BOEING COMMERCIAL AIRPLANES

Created in 2005, Boeing's Airplane Production organization combines the former
Supplier Management organization with all commercial airplane production activities
in Everett, Auburn, and Renton, Washington, and Long Beach, California. At the
time of the project, Carolyn Corvi, was responsible for managing Boeing Commercial
Airplanes' fully integrated production system, from design through production and
delivery. Prior to this assignment, Corvi was Vice President and General Manager of
the 737/757 programs. Under her leadership, the 737/757 programs incorporated
industry-leading applications of lean manufacturing principles. Corvi joined Boeing
in 1974 and has held a variety of key leadership assignments. For her contributions
to both the company and aerospace industry, Corvi won the 2001 Women in
Aerospace Leadership award. She currently serves on Virginia Mason Medical
Center's Health System Board of Directors and is on the president's advisory board
at Embry-Riddle Aeronautical University.

**Let's start by talking about the Boeing 737. when this project began you were
the vice president in charge of the Boeing 737 programs. What is the history
of that plane in the marketplace?** The 737 has a long history at Boeing that
goes back to 1967. Completely redesigned 10 years ago, today's 737 is called the
Next Generation 737 and it's part of the Boeing tradition of designing airplane
families. The 737 family includes the 737-600, the 737-700, the 737-800 and the
737-900ER. In dual-class configuration, the 737-600 seats 110 people and the
737-900ER, for example, seats 180 but can seat up to 215 people in a single class.
It's a very capable family of airplanes. It's the longest running and best-selling
commercial jet in history with more than 6,000 sold and we continue to be very
competitive in this size of airplane.

**When you first started thinking about the idea of rebuilding the facility at
Renton, what were the opportunities and challenges that the 737 program was
facing?** In 2001, as the year began, the market conditions were quite strong. We
were selling into an up market and demand was high. But then a confluence of
local and world events happened that had a major impact on business. We had an
earthquake in the area in February 2001 which damaged several of our buildings.
September 11th changed security in airports and, as we all know, had a significant
impact on the airline industry. Later in 2003, the SARS epidemic in Asia, more
terrorist attacks, and the war in Iraq were all detrimental to the industry.

IF THERE'S A PROBLEM WITH A PRODUCT, IT'S NOT THE MECHANIC'S RESPONSIBILITY OR THE INSPECTOR'S OR THE SUPERVISOR'S. IT'S THE ENTIRE TEAM'S.

So we went from a boom of the early part of 2001, when we started to think about how we could transform the work environment for our people, to the bust at the end of the year. That rapid business downturn and the uncertainty about when it would bounce back gave us even more reason to change. We were faced with an opportunity. We didn't relish the situation, because of all the external conditions forced on us, but it was the perfect time to do something different. We knew we could take advantage of the downtime in the marketplace.

At the time that all of these factors were coming together, the 737s were being assembled in the facility at Renton that Boeing had been using since the 1960s. What was the factory like? The Renton factory was a vast building with high bays, cement floors, exposed structural beams, and open mezzanine storage areas for parts and tools. We used overhead cranes to move parts of the airplanes and heavy equipment around the factory. As we began to lean out our processes, things began to visibly change and when we moved to a just-in-time production system, our inventory levels in the factory went down and this freed up the mezzanine storage areas.

At the same time, an earthquake in February 2001 destroyed the office building that our engineers worked in and we scrambled to move 1,400 engineers and support staff to temporary locations. Under normal conditions, a move of 1,400 people would have been a major undertaking, but the facilities staff pulled this off over a weekend.

These two things happening at the same time led us to think about how we could use all the assets on the site more efficiently. We asked ourselves: how do we create a way to help people work more productively, meet our vision of a leaner production system, and use the space that we have on the site better without rebuilding the engineering building?

So we started to think about moving everyone into the factory. It's something I had wanted to do since 1989, when I worked in manufacturing engineering. I frequently heard from factory workers that design engineers didn't come to the factory often enough.

Yes, you've called this "the tragedy of classical manufacturing." The tragedy of classical manufacturing is that designers are separated from assemblers. We've learned from Japanese manufacturers that there are gains when the engineers who support ongoing production live on the factory floor. If there's a problem with a product, it's not the mechanic's responsibility or the inspector's or the supervisor's. It's the entire team of people led by the engineer who designed it. If you design something you should be responsible for whether or not somebody can build it.

The real opportunity for Renton was to change the way people worked together. The idea was to bring everybody together around the product, because everything that we do here is about the plane. If we don't sell airplanes, there's really no reason for any of us to come to work each day. If we don't produce the kinds of airplanes that our customers want to keep buying, there's no future. Getting everybody's attention focused on the airplane, and on the customer associated with that airplane, was, and still is, the primary goal.

PROJECT PROFILE

One of four operating groups within The Boeing Company, Commercial Airplanes is headquartered in Renton, Washington. It is organized into three primary business units—Airplane Program, the 787 Dreamliner Program, and Commercial Aviation Services—operating out of Renton and Everett, Washington, and Long Beach, California.

The Boeing 737 is the most widely used commercial jetliner in history, accounting for nearly one-third of all commercial jetliners in service. Each day, the more than 4,000 737s that are in service worldwide carry a combined total of about 1.3 million passengers. Every 4.6 seconds, a 737 takes off or lands somewhere on the globe.

Boeing's 278-acre Renton site encompasses 4.1 million square feet (380,902 square meters) of building space. Throughout the years, Renton has been home to many of commercial aviation's best known airplanes, including the 707, 727, and the original models of the 737 and 757. Today, employees there produce the popular Boeing Next Generation 737.

The ground floor of the final assembly building for the Boeing 737 covers 760,000 square feet (70,600 square meters)—approximately two city blocks. Activities at other main buildings at the Renton site include wing-line production and a paint hangar.

Boeing became the first commercial airframe manufacturer to use a moving assembly line to build jetliners when the production lines were transformed from semi-stationary production lines to a continuously moving line. The airplanes on the line move continuously at a rate of two inches (five centimeters) per minute; the line stops only for employee breaks, critical production issues, or shift changes.

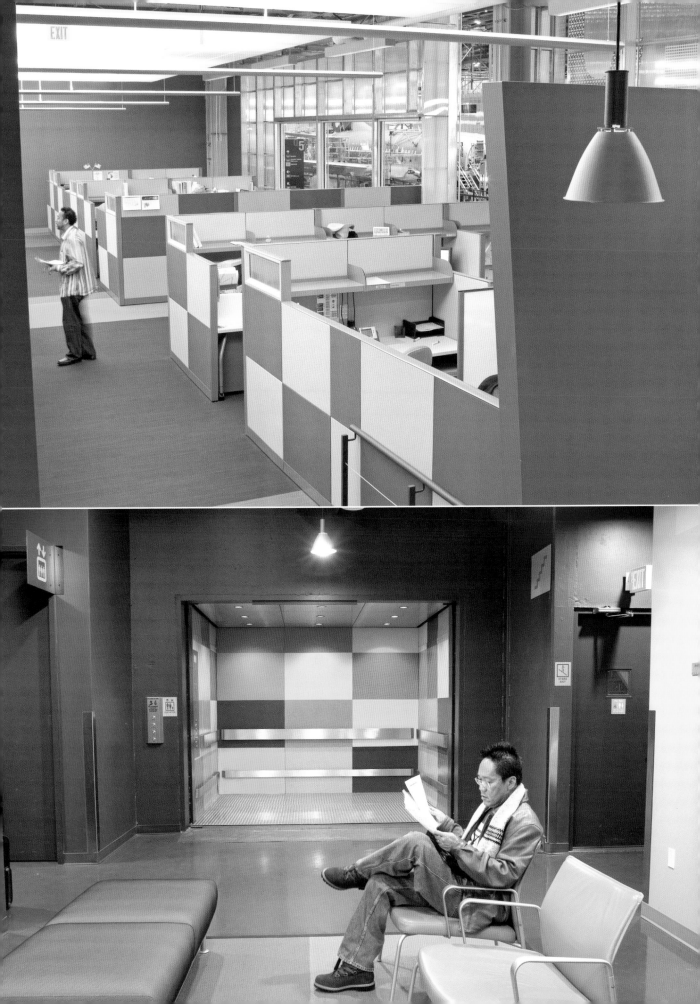

22 DAYS
1999, BEFORE LEAN
AND RENOVATION

11 DAYS
2006, AFTER LEAN
AND RENOVATION

LEAN MANUFACTURING:
The moving line was one of several techniques
introduced as part of the adoption of "lean
manufacturing" principles. Lean practice involves
changing a work area or a business process to
maximize efficiency, improve quality and safety,
eliminate unnecessary motion and inventory, and
save time. Lean manufacturing efforts have
decreased Boeing's production time for commercial
airplanes from 22 to 11 days.

How did you approach the challenge of breaking this tradition of separation? It
came together through a number of different events. I had been to the Starbucks
world headquarters in Seattle and was struck by how they designed all their
corporate office space to look like their retail stores. I wanted to do something
similar—to capture what we do here at Boeing and make our offices an extension
of that, a place where people really get excited about what we do.

It was clearly important never to lose sight of the fact that we couldn't
create a work environment in the factory that disenfranchised the people who had
traditionally worked in the factory. We couldn't create the haves and the have-nots.
We couldn't forget that it was a factory and that we were here to build airplanes.

We used the term "industrial cool" to talk about the environment we were
trying to create. We didn't want to change what was there—the steel beams and the
corrugated metal walls—we just wanted to make it livable for everyone. A key to
that was what we called "the right to light"— we punched windows into the exterior
walls to bring natural light into a space that traditionally shuts it out entirely.

So the goals were to make it a good place to come to work, a fun place,
but not different from what it had been before. It would be designed in a way
that made it acceptable for everybody to do their job, recognizing that people
have different needs.

**Once the design team was in place, a pilot project was launched. How did
that idea come about?** We were inspired by the idea that we had moved 1,400
engineers and support staff over a weekend. You have to work in a big company
to know how hard that would be to do if you planned it. The business of building
airplanes is cyclical and we knew that if we were going to make a big change, the
best time to do it was when we were in a downturn. We created a small pilot area.
It was like a model showroom. We placed notices in our internal publications so
people could go and check out the space and we asked for feedback about working in an area like that. This let people know that something was going to happen
that was different.

We followed that up by moving a group of 40 volunteers, all engineers, into
the factory, placing them on the mezzanine with just traditional office furniture.

Did they have any kind of hesitations? They thought it was an interesting idea
until the birds started flying in and landing on their desks. It wasn't an optimal
situation. The lighting wasn't very good. The engineers had to walk down three
flights of stairs to help the mechanics with the airplanes. At the end of a 60-day
stay, we told the engineers that they could move back—and none of them wanted
to leave. They all stayed and said, "This is much better," despite the conditions
they were working in. It really gave us hope.

At first everybody had been sensitive to the idea that engineers wouldn't
want to work in that environment. They're used to quiet cubicles, privacy, and
carpets. We also learned along the way that the mechanics, who for years had said,
"You know, the engineers never come to the factory to help us," were intimidated
by the prospect of 1,400 engineers moving to the factory. People were moving into
"their house," so they started to get nervous too. We worked very carefully to
make sure that everybody knew what the expectations were and that we were
being respectful of everybody's work habits.

How did you create a space that put those fears to rest for both groups? We
talked extensively with NBBJ about collaboration. They developed a concept where
the factory floor was treated like a showroom. They built the office-tower walls
out of translucent polycarbonate panels and transparent glazing. It's very open,
so one of the things that we talked about was the idea that when people sit in

their cubicles or office space on these mezzanine levels looking out at the factory, it couldn't be like a fishbowl. We didn't want everyone on the floor feeling like everybody up above was staring at them. NBBJ came up with the idea of interspersing glass with the opaque Lexan. The light comes through it, you can see shapes, but it's not transparent like glass. There is some privacy; at the same time there's a tremendous amount of connectivity. It works well as a way of celebrating what we do and making a direct connection between the planes and the knowledge behind them.

As people started to move into the factory over a series of months, we started to form neighborhood associations, almost like a Welcome Wagon. We made a point of bringing the engineering groups down to the factory floor, pairing them up with the people who worked on the airplane or who installed the parts that they designed. We also had the mechanics go up and see where the engineers sat. By walking into each other's space they partnered together to try to break down the barriers between them.

You started this project off with the idea that there were productivity gains that you could make, and ways in which this could work with your lean process. How have you been able to measure the achievements of this facility?

CHANGE DESIGN
TOOL IN ACTION

LET VISION DRIVE THE PROGRAMMING

Accomplishing change with architectural design starts by tying the needs of the architectural program to the vision for the organization. That's why the tool NBBJ has developed to ensure that happens is called "Let Vision Drive the Programming." This tool helped get to the heart of Boeing's vision for the transformation of its Renton site by assessing behavior, work patterns, future goals, and trends alongside practical space needs.

SEE PAGE 180 FOR MORE INFORMATION ABOUT THIS TOOL.

AN AWESOME ASSEMBLY LINE

Boeing's commitment to continuous improvement in assembly processes means the workplace environment has to enable groups to reassemble as processes evolve. Early on, and all through the design process, we spent time with a cross section of individuals within the organization to get to know their current lean work practices. The goal was to come up with a framework that would enable the workplace culture to continually evolve. The framework ended up emphasizing two aspects: it's all about the plane; it's all about the people.

So, from virtually any place in the office environment, you never lose sight of the airplanes moving through the assembly line. The collaborative spaces are always oriented towards the plane. You are simultaneously a participant and a spectator in creating the world's best airplanes. As a design

team, we were inspired and in awe of the assembly process. We wanted to make this amazing and continuous transformation, from parts at one end to a completed airplane at the other, really visible to everyone. That was a critical aspect of how Boeing's vision drove our programming and design. Standing in the office environment of this 1,000-foot-long, 100-foot-high building, seeing each airplane come together in front of your eyes, makes a big and very positive impression. It makes the familiar new, and that's a real morale booster.

ANNE CUNNINGHAM, PRINCIPAL, NBBJ

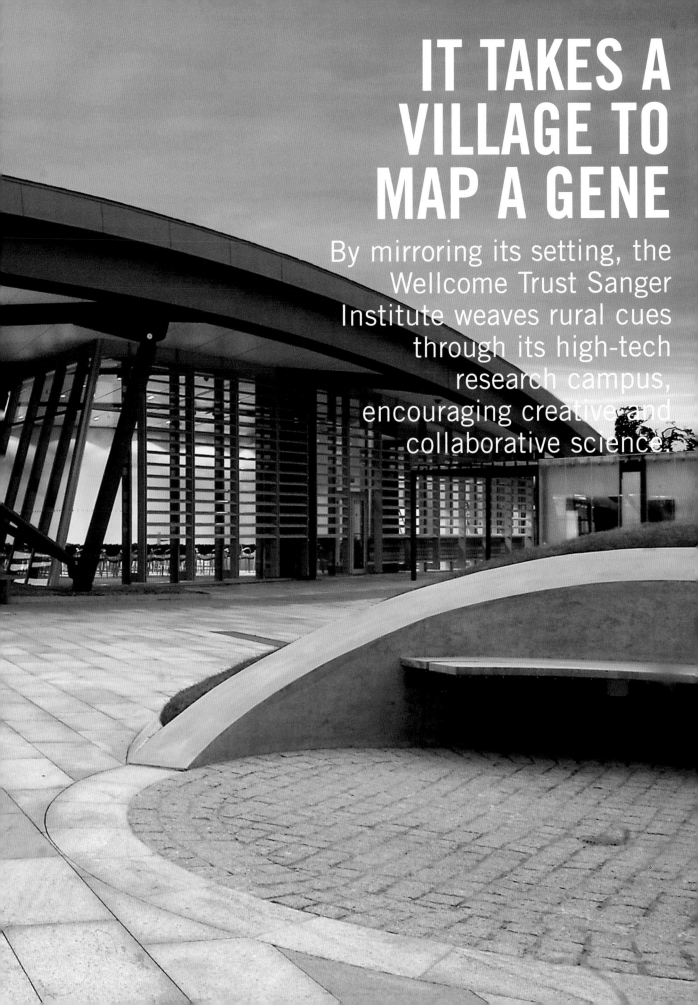

IT TAKES A VILLAGE TO MAP A GENE

By mirroring its setting, the Wellcome Trust Sanger Institute weaves rural cues through its high-tech research campus, encouraging creative and collaborative science.

JOHN COOPER

DIRECTOR OF RESOURCES, WELLCOME TRUST

As well as being the Director of Resources for the Wellcome Trust in London, U.K., John Cooper is also Managing Director of the Wellcome Trust Genome Campus near Cambridge, U.K. He is responsible for a wide range of business services, including HR, IT, and Facilities Management, as well as several large capital projects, including the Genome Campus expansion. He also manages the Wellcome Trust Conference Centres on the Genome Campus and in London, and an interesting and fast-growing program of advanced genomics training courses for post-doctoral researchers. Before joining the Trust in 1999, Cooper spent 30 years in the commercial electronics industry, formerly as a main board director of a U.K. public company with extensive business interests in the U.S.A. and Europe.

Let's start by talking about Wellcome Trust itself. We are a research funding organization. Particularly in the U.K., a lot of people remember that there was a drug company called Wellcome or Glaxo-Wellcome, and we were confused with them regularly, so we always make the point that we're a charitable foundation, not a drug company. We fund research, mainly research carried out in universities and research institutes. For instance, we're the major non-U.S. funder of the Human Genome Project. We fund a lot of research into tropical medicine, malaria and HIV/AIDS, and tuberculosis, and a lot of basic blue-sky biological research, often in the U.K. universities. Our goal is the public good; our mission is to promote research with the aim of improving human and animal health.

You are dedicated not just to research, but also to applied research. Yes, we do some applied research—probably not as much as we would like to. We take the view that we should not try to do what the commercial world can do as well or better, but there are gaps in the process of translating fundamental research into healthcare benefits that we believe we can fill. Usually it's very early-stage investment in promising ideas. When the market is ready to take them up, then we pull out.

You mentioned the Wellcome Trust involvement in the Human Genome Project, and you are chief executive of the Wellcome Trust Genome Campus. Can you recap the role that Wellcome Trust has played in the Human Genome Project? Through the Wellcome Trust Sanger Institute, we funded about 35 percent of the international effort on the Human Genome Project. The other major contribution

MOST BRITISH SCIENCE IS CARRIED OUT IN UNIVERSITIES OR IN CITY CENTERS, OFTEN IN OLD BUILDINGS. WE'VE CREATED A LOVELY RURAL CAMPUS WITH MODERN BUILDINGS.

we made is our insistence that the results of the research be published immediately, so that whatever sequence had been discovered during the day was put on the Internet that evening. We insisted that if we were to be involved in the project the results had to be made freely available to scientists anywhere in the world. And that, of course, goes straight to our mission.

Can you describe the original campus where that work was done? Until, I think, about the Second World War, it was a country estate, Hinxton Hall, an 18th century country house with 125 acres of land.

During the war, Hinxton Hall was used by the U.S. Air Force as accommodation for pilots from the nearby U.S. air base at Duxford. After the war it was converted into a research center by a British engineering group. They pulled out. It was lying unused and not in great condition in the early 1990s, when we were looking for somewhere to start up work on the Human Genome Project. So, we bought it. Initially people worked out of the old buildings, and then in the mid-1990s we built some new laboratories.

Wellcome Trust first applied to expand the campus in the late 1990s. What was the original intent? The original purpose, actually, was to build an innovation center and some grow-on spaces for small genomics companies, the idea being to develop a science park around the genomics facility. And we were unable to get planning consent for that, after many public inquiries. In the meantime, we came under increasing pressure for space for academic research facilities, so we had a change of plan. We split the project into two parts. Phase One was to build more academic space. Phase Two would be to build the innovation center—or incubator, as everyone calls it—and commercial space.

So far, all we have done is build the academic space. The world has moved on and the biotech sector is not doing particularly well. So, we're waiting until we believe that there's a reasonable demand for genomics start-up activities before we make a decision on building Phase Two.

What motivated the opposition that you talked about to the original plans? I think it was concern about development in greenfield sites. Cambridge is an area that has grown very fast (by U.K. standards, not by the standards of Silicon Valley) and the infrastructure has not kept pace, so there are problems with roads and schools—perceived problems; probably nothing compared to some major U.S. cities, or indeed London. But Cambridge is a very beautiful university city in a very pleasant rural area, nice rolling countryside, and a lot of people wanted to keep it that way. I live in that area myself, so in many ways I agree with them.

But, in point of fact, when we went back with our revised proposal, which was four to five years on from the original proposal, we had no problem. There'd been a lot of local debate, a lot of discussion between ourselves and the planning authorities, and I have to say that the planning authorities and the local community

50 PERCENT OF ROOFS ON CAMPUS ARE COVERED IN SEDUM

were very cooperative. I think what had happened in the meantime was people had seen the tremendous achievements of the Sanger Institute and the Human Genome Project and they actually felt proud to be associated with it. Five years before that, of course, it was a bit of an unknown, and it was going to be a very commercial development. Now it was a research development to take further work of which the local communities themselves had become justifiably proud.

How did those initial concerns of the surrounding communities influence the design approach? We tried to make sure that the buildings were as unobtrusive as possible, so they're low buildings, maximum two stories. The two biggest buildings have green roofs, and the roofs slope down towards one of the villages, so if the residents are looking at the site from where they live what they actually see is a plant called sedum—they see a large sedum roof, they see flowers.

So that was one response. Another response was to make sure that what we did had a positive environmental impact. Around the edge of the site is a small river that flooded regularly, and there was concern that the runoff from new buildings might exacerbate those problems. We built a 15-acre wetland, so that when the river overflowed it flowed into this wetland, which we turned into a nature reserve. It's only been operating for about a year, but already otters have returned to breed in the area, and some interesting birds. It will take five to 10 years to reach anything like maturity, but when it does it will be a very nice small nature reserve.

We also tried to use materials for the buildings that fitted with the local style, so, for instance, a number of the walls of the buildings are made of flint stones embedded in concrete panels so it looks like a flint wall, which there are a lot of in the local villages.

PROJECT PROFILE

The Wellcome Trust Sanger Institute is one of the world's pre-eminent genome research centers. It is best known as the single largest contributor to the global Human Genome Project.

Funding is primarily provided by the Wellcome Trust, Europe's largest biomedical research charity with investments of $20 billion.

The project includes a master plan for the extended campus. Development is planned in three phases. The first includes an expansion to Sanger Institute academic/laboratory buildings, a super-computing data center, and campus amenities. Future phases include an innovation center for startup businesses and facilities for spin-offs.

The institute's cancer genome project is among the world's largest cancer genome studies. It searches for genetic mutations that cause the most common cancers, including breast, lung, colorectal, ovarian, and prostate.

Located on a 51-hectare (125-acre) campus in Hinxton, Cambridge, the existing labs accommodated 650 staff. This 291,000-square-foot (27,000-square-meter) campus extension allows the institute to add up to 200 more scientists.

In its first seven years, the staff size of the Sanger Institute increased from 15 to 580. Eighty percent of the staff live within 16 kilometers (10 miles) of the campus, although they are recruited from more than 20 countries around the world.

The sustainable campus achieved the U.K.'s BREEAM, "Very Good" equivalent rating for science facilities.

As much as possible we built underground parking. The surface car parking is hidden behind grass banks with trees and shrubs on the top. So, we've tried to make the buildings blend in with the local environment.

Obviously these features have a tremendous effect on people who are outside the campus. Do they affect the people who are on the campus? As you can imagine, working in 125 acres of parkland, there's a very nice working environment. Most British science is carried out in universities or in city centers, and often in pretty old buildings. The environment that we've created is of a lovely rural campus with classy modern buildings on it. It certainly makes me feel good to go there.

The other thing that we've done is we've built the Cairns Pavilion, which has a new staff restaurant and a small sports hall. You can use it to play badminton and other things. We also have built a new football [soccer] pitch—very important in the U.K. So we've gone a long way to improve the facilities for people, and already we've seen a big increase in the use of these facilities. The takings in the staff restaurant have shot up compared with what we had before, simply because it's a nice place.

And what are you hoping the spin-off effects will be in terms of people's creativity and productivity? What one always hopes is that by encouraging interaction between researchers working in different groups you get a cross-fertilization of ideas. You've got groups of people doing very basic science, and you've got other groups of people studying particular disease types, and clearly one hopes that these people are swapping notes and learning from each other. I don't know whether we've got any evidence, yet, that that's happened, but that's certainly one of our objectives: encouraging informal interaction between people to improve the creativity of the place.

There is a lot of evidence that organizations that work informally, work better. I'm speaking to you from our head office in London, which we've just finished, and we moved from having half our staff working in cellular offices to having all but 10 or 12 people working in open offices, and already the level of interaction has increased incredibly because, you know, they can now see and meet each other. And it's the same process in the case of the campus applied to a research environment.

As part of the expansion you had to do some recruiting from amongst the world's top scientists. How do you design and build for that sort of need? What we did first of all, of course, was to work with the people who were already there. We built good laboratory space but we built to a standard approach. Then, of course, as the new scientists started appearing, the space had to be customized, and so we were building and customizing almost at the same time. Which is fine; the way the whole project was designed and procured gave us that flexibility. So we started off not really knowing exactly what would be needed by many of the scientists, and then gradually adjusted the design along the way to give them what they needed.

On the subject of how things can be adjusted as you go along, you mentioned that the second phase of the project at this point is on hold, pending developments in the wider world. How will you be able to move on to that second phase if you need to? What we built in the first phase is actually six different buildings, and with our master plan we would put up new additional buildings on land which is immediately adjacent to what we've already built. It's easy to expand.

In some ways this new campus is an experiment in a new way of working, and that seems fitting for a scientific institute, but what made it an experiment that

CHANGE DESIGN
TOOL IN ACTION

DESIGN THE PROCESS / BUILD TOUCHSTONES

Designing not only structures but change requires a set of tools that are not only non-traditional but flexible. Because every client challenge, and site is unique, it's just as important to design the process for a project as it is to design the project. NBBJ uses a number of tools to design the process, including one called "Build Touchstones," which kept Wellcome Trust's new campus on course by identifying the projects, and the organization's, guiding principles.

SEE PAGE 202 FOR MORE INFORMATION ABOUT THIS TOOL.

RURAL ROOTS

Touchstones act as a reference, a criterion guiding, directing, and focusing a design team's efforts. The inspiration for this tool came from Cirque du Soleil. When they put on a production, they come up with an initial concept, and as they start to do their lighting design, their set design, their choreography, their acts, everything has to support that one concept. If it doesn't, it's thrown out. You get stronger design that way. You're never caught in a situation where someone's saying, "Well, I just did it because I like it that way." Everything's supporting a general concept that supports the project.

On Wellcome Trust, the Number One rule was to take cues from the landscape and the area. Secondary was the idea that where you had people-focused functions, those environments were going to take their cues from nature, and where the focus of the work was more scientific in nature, those areas were going to be more man-made. By coming up with that concrete set of rules from the very beginning, every time a question would arise about how to treat a certain area, you could always go back to that concept and say, "Okay, this is what to do." It was great for the design team and for the user groups, because when anyone said, "Why are we doing it that way?" the reply was "Remember our concept. This is how these things are ordered."

JONATHAN WARD, PARTNER, NBBJ

you felt was worth undertaking? Well, I suppose two things. You really do have to believe that the quality of work that you're doing there is important, and I think everybody believes that the work that was done on the Human Genome Project, the work that's now going on, is really high quality and very important. Secondly, you have to believe that creative people can spark ideas off each other if you put them together in the sort of environment where they can have relatively casual interaction with each other. And that all seems right, it seems sensible, it doesn't seem far-fetched to believe that creative people working together will generate good ideas, so it's a matter of building an environment which facilitates that. You can't make it happen, but you can build something that will allow it to happen. So I suppose it's a bit of an act of faith, but it seems a pretty good bet.

Allan Bradley became Director of the Sanger Institute in November 2000. Under his leadership, the institute has appointed more than 20 new faculty researchers to capitalize on genomic research for understanding biology, human health, and disease. In July 2002, he was elected Fellow of the Royal Society. Prior to joining the Sanger, Bradley was a professor at the Baylor College of Medicine in Houston, Texas. He completed his PhD studies in genetics at the University of Cambridge in 1984, where he co-developed the embryonic stem cell system.

PROFESSOR ALLAN BRADLEY
DIRECTOR, WELLCOME TRUST SANGER INSTITUTE

You took over as director of the Sanger Institute at about the same time as the project to expand the campus began. What were your initial thoughts about the project, especially in relation to what you hoped to do as director? When I arrived, this campus had a very single, clear mission, which was decoding the human genome. The mission that is unfolding now is about not just understanding what all those letters encode but what that code really means, so it's about the function of genes.

And so from a campus that deployed a single technology—genome sequencing—it's now going to be a campus that has a much more diverse infrastructure need. So that meant more high-spec space in terms of molecular biology, more space for animal experiments, and a lot more space for a computing infrastructure.

What you're doing has been described as bringing biology to the genome. You know, some people refer to the genome as the book of life, but what you have to remember is that it is a book with a million pages of text when printed out, and so what we need to do is understand what is on those pages and what it is there for: why is that sequence there, what happens if something goes wrong, how is it important in health, and how is it important in disease? Just having information is extremely important, but you have to go beyond, you have to use it.

And so our mission is really two-fold. We are adding value to that sequence, or bringing biology to the genome, if you like, but we also are sharing that information with the community at large. A very big part of our mission—and has been from the start—is giving away information about the sequence, helping people do their experiments on-line using our computer infrastructure, and sharing data we generate ourselves with external users as well.

How equipped were you to be able to take those next steps within the original campus? In some ways we were extremely restricted. For example, even when this building, the Sulston Laboratories, I'm in was built and finished—in 1996, I think—they had significantly underestimated the requirement for the computing infrastructure in order to deliver information to the world.

The design for the new campus is very different from what has been on the grounds up until now. How did Sanger scientists initially view the design concept? We were heavily consulted and heavily involved in the design at all levels, including answering questions about whether we wanted it to be a single building or multiple buildings. Obviously, most of the ideas were brought to us by the architects, but they were bounced off us in a series of meetings, to make sure that we and the architects and engineers really truly agreed as to what we were trying to build.

What were some of the key ideas that came up through that consultative process? Well, I think one of the things they wanted to do was move the heart of the campus a little bit away from where it was, so the key thing was to build a building where people in the new buildings would interact with the people in the existing building. For an institute it's very important that different groups of people know what is going on in different areas of the research enterprise; there's a lot of science that is nucleated by casual connection—you know, sitting down and having a cup of coffee, or bumping into one another in the hall or in an open space somewhere. And it's actually quite hard, I think, to make that happen when we're spread out over quite a lot of space. The new building, I think, really

has enabled that to occur not only within the groups in the building, but also between the people in that building and other parts of the campus.

There's an area of the new campus called the market square. How does that function? The market square is a space between the cafeteria, the coffee shop, and the sports facility on one side, and the offices of the research building on the other. Behind it are the research buildings and the supercomputing data center. And then to one side is the existing Sanger Building, now called the Sulston Laboratories. So in terms of its location it's not quite a quadrant, but the view was that it would be a place where paths would cross and connect—you know, the market square. And in fact the entrance to the carpark comes right out in the middle of the market square, so that's another dimension that was designed to make people meet each other in the morning, because you would see people going for coffee, or going into the buildings, or going to the gym or whatever. There's nobody selling vegetables or anything like that! It's just kind of a meeting place. And people do meet casually and, if the weather's fine, they'll even stand out and discuss things. So it's a little bit like an Italian piazza.

That idea of science coming out of casual interaction, is that an accepted truth in the scientific community? I think it is, absolutely, yes. I think you see it in modern science buildings, and also you see it in the old ones. If you go into the old science buildings in Cambridge, that meeting place is actually the tea room. Now, it's not often built into an American science building, a tea room. So they tend to build smaller, little casual areas. But the cafeteria never really compensates for a tea room.

What is the tea room at Cambridge? Well, in any academic building in Cambridge there'll be a tea room where tea and coffee are served in the morning at 10:30 and tea is served at 3:30 in the afternoon, and people will gather for a tea break. You can go to a room where most of the occupants of the building will be at that period in time, and so you can actually get a lot of business done in that 20 minutes, rather than trading phone calls and e-mails and that kind of stuff. So it's casual, but it's not casual in terms of what it's delivering, which is important information exchange between individuals.

And have you been able to replicate that with the new facilities? Yes, and indeed in the old ones. In fact, when the architects first came here they recognized one of the successes of the current building was that there was a very popular tea room that was called The DINA. And so they've built a similar sort of coffee bar, the Pebble Cafe, in the new building as another nucleus for people to gather.

You are just newly into the building, but can you see evidence of it working? Oh, yes. I can see it working. But one of the other aspects of the design is rather than having labs with walls, the laboratory space is a very open plan, so there are different groups who are literally back to back, whereas in previous buildings they would have had walls dividing them up. So it means that information is flowing, because people are almost in the same space, if you like; they're sharing the lab and they're sharing the materials and they're sharing ideas.

And that comes back to things like how we deal with our data, how we share our data. We can have a bigger impact than people who do their experiments in their laboratories and then eventually put them into the scientific literature. Because we do that immediately, we have a much bigger impact, we think, than people who are more secretive about the work they're doing. And the building does support that way of working. You know, buildings without walls don't lend to secrecy.

How unusual is it to have the kind of transparency you're describing, in a lab environment? I think it's relatively unusual. When I was working in the States, there were no labs in the States that I was aware of that were built that way, certainly not in Baylor [Baylor College of Medicine, Houston, Texas], where I was previously. They'd built a lot of labs over the 15 years I was there, but they never embraced the open-lab concept. People tended to like to have four walls and a door they could lock at night, whereas here that's impossible because the space is shared with lots of other people.

And given that it was a bit different, how did people feel about the open-lab concept when it was originally introduced? Initially, there was a little bit of trepidation about moving into that environment, but I've heard many people say to me, just in the past month, "It's amazing. Our productivity's increased since we've moved." Considering one is moving into a new building, with all of the upset that causes, just getting things organized, it's quite interesting that they already feel a positive impact.

It has also allowed a lot of flexibility in terms of managing the space, which was the other primary reason for doing it. If you're putting up walls, eventually you're going to have to take them down or move them, and we didn't want to have to deal with that. So it's very modular, it can be shifted around, benches can be taken out and other things can be put in if necessary. It's designed with flexibility—long-term flexibility—in mind.

Which is something that would be important, given the way the Institute is shifting its interest? Yes. Certainly my view is that science doesn't stand still, and shouldn't stand still. It'll move and we should move with it.

Since 1993, Phil Butcher has overseen the development of the Sanger Institute's Information Technology infrastructure. He manages a team of 50 people providing networks, databases, web services, and the high-performance infrastructure necessary for the institute. Before the Sanger, Butcher worked in the commercial sector for more than 12 years where he managed and developed IT systems at an R&D software house. He also provided IT consultancy services across Europe and the U.S.

PHIL BUTCHER
HEAD OF INFORMATION TECHNOLOGY, WELLCOME TRUST SANGER INSTITUTE

You're head of IT for the Sanger Institute. What's the importance of information technology in this type of scientific setting? The Sanger Institute has been, for the past 13 years, pretty much devoted to sequencing human DNA, which is made up of three billion base pairs or chemicals. End to end they are very similar in each human, and a very small fraction are different, which gives us different color eyes, height, hair, and so on. Our whole aim was to take human DNA and be able to put the sequence of chemicals in a row so you could read, from one end to the other, the three billion base pairs. The chemicals are adenine, cytosine, thiamine, and guanine, which is computationally represented by A, C, T, and G, so what we have to do is get those As, Cs, Ts, and Gs and put them in the right order for three billion characters made up of just those four bases.

So, do the math! It's a huge computational effort to do that in the first place. But it's been achieved. Since we started this endeavor in 1993–94, the Sanger Institute has contributed more and more complete DNA to the public domain database than any other organization in the world.

Now we're sequencing other genomes, of other organisms like zebra fish and mice. We have 10 to 20 genomes available on our web site, so one can be compared with the other to find differences and similarities, so that we can understand how humans are made up, which inevitably will lead us into understanding how we can apply that to medicine, and how we can treat particular hereditary diseases.

One of the main goals of the institute's new campus is to better enable data emerging from the genome work to be translated into practical health benefits. How can data processing help achieve that goal? Much of the science now depends on the computational side to analyze the data. If you have three billion base pairs—and that's just one genome—and you want to compare it to another genome, that's three billion against three billion base pairs. You can't do that without very high-scale, high-performance computers.

So in some essential way, the computational work is the science, or is a large part of the science? Exactly. It's an integral part. Genomic-based science cannot be done without a very decent computational infrastructure.

Over the years, we have grown a very large, high-performance computing infrastructure—300,000 gigabytes. If you think, in your PC you may have a 40 gigabyte disk. We have thousands of CPUs working on these problems. We've had up to 400 machines in a rack, and when you have that much computer power in a single space, not only does it draw a lot of power, but it also outputs an awful lot of heat. You can't just switch these things on in an office and hope for the best. It means you need a radical design for how you're going to deal with these heat loads. The idea of providing a computer room is a very, very serious business for us.

Given what you've been talking about, it's interesting that when you were asked what you would like in a new data center—or computer room, to put it simply—you specified a computing capacity that was, per square meter, still two to three times greater than the industry standard. Why were you setting your sights so high? Our main problem is that we always outgrow the environment. The industry in general hasn't been able to build systems that are really future-proof for a good, long while.

You have to take into consideration as well the differences between machine rooms in the U.S. and machine rooms in the U.K. and Europe. In the

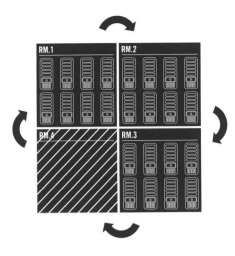

TECHNOLOGY REFRESH:
The data center is organized into four identical rooms on a single floor. It houses some of the U.K.'s most powerful computers and every year approximately 15% of its computers are replaced for newer, faster equipment. Due to this high turnover, one room is always rotated "off-line" so equipment can be decommissioned and refreshed every two to four years.

U.S., where space is easier to come by, people tend to build larger machine rooms, and therefore the power, heat, and density problems are less. In the U.K. and Europe, where we don't have so much free space, the parcels of land we're given to build on tend to be smaller. We are trying to do very high capacity computing on a smaller footprint. Therefore, the heat and power density problems are more relevant to us.

The new campus has many elements to it, but the data center was determined to be the riskiest part of the entire project. Why was that? There were a lot of unknowns. Originally, the design was to look at traditional computer room air conditioning units. While that's the regular way of cooling machine rooms, it's not necessarily, in our opinion, the most cost-effective or efficient way to do it these days. Early on in the project, we went to review other data centers around the world and in the U.S. to see what technologies they were using, and we came across fan coil technology, which is what we eventually deployed, modified to fit our needs.

It hasn't been widely used elsewhere, particularly in this way, so we set up room simulations using "computational fluid dynamic modeling" (CFD), and then actually built real setups that were doing research to see whether it was valid for us to go ahead. Yes, it was very risky, but we took the steps to prove the technology. We were reasonably comfortable with what we'd seen and what we could do, but the actual proving of it had to be done in parallel with the machine room being built.

You mentioned the tour that you went on. One of the major epiphanies of the project occurred on a plane ride between data centers. What happened? We spent quite a lot of time in the air between various cities in order to look at these installations. So it did end up as an awful lot of time in airplane gangways, discussing on scraps of paper and laptops, with all of us pitching in and coming up with ideas about what would and wouldn't be workable.

We'd decided that we were going to build four quadrants, or four machine rooms, so that we could actually isolate some of the kit, rather than just building one big, 1,000-square-meter room.

One of the ideas that we came up with on the plane was that we should keep one of the four machine rooms empty so that if I do outgrow the environment we could actually refurbish the technology in there to accommodate machines that have yet to be invented. I'm not going to fill all these rooms at day one, and I have to build capacity in for expansion; otherwise, what's the point of building? If you're going to put spare capacity in, why not actually build the spare capacity? Why don't you just put the shell in and leave us the maximum amount of flexibility that we could possibly hope to have? It's what I call "the fallow field principle."

It's interesting to think of that agricultural terminology applied in such a highly technical environment. It seems suitable for a campus that is right in the middle of a pastoral area. It's true. I went to bed one night on the trip and woke up, and I thought, it's obvious. People have done this in ancient agricultural terms for years. Why not deploy this within our setting? I have a rotating crop. My crop just happens to be IT.

And actually, we save money, because we haven't filled a quarter of the building, which probably we may well have done, had we gone for the traditional method. But we decided to do this thing. So it saved money, it gave us future proofing, real future proofing and flexibility. It has yet to be proven, but we're quietly confident.

One of your other major challenges, as you touched on earlier, was heat and cooling. In the course of figuring out how you were going to solve that, the design team talked about sticking an ice cube on top of the computers—another metaphor. What did it turn into? Well, originally the idea was that we were going to have one floor of computer rooms, and the two floors above it were going to be full of the air conditioning systems. It was going to take a huge amount of space, so it became nicknamed "the ice cube," because we had this huge, square block sitting on top of a very thin layer of machines underneath.

But of course what happened was that we moved to this fan coil system, which was installed within the machine rooms, so we could actually reorder the space that we had upstairs. Now, not only do I have an empty fourth quadrant, I actually have spare capacity within the plant rooms upstairs so that if I want to, I can put in an additional chiller plant to accommodate the fourth room. We really do have a huge amount of flexibility in that bit we called the ice cube. To top it off, they did put blue glass all around the outside of the building, so it does look a bit like an ice cube.

It's interesting how metaphors have a way of influencing physicality. What are the effects of having a building that creates so much heat actually look like an ice cube? I think what it does do, actually—because it would normally be concrete—you only have to look at the building, and you suddenly realize how much effort it takes to cool modern day computer systems. They don't all just sit in offices. It does give an impression, I guess, to the outside world, of the kind of efforts we have to go to to support the science that we do.

EUROPEAN BIOINFORMATICS INSTITUTE

In addition to the Sanger Institute, the Wellcome Trust Genome Campus is home to another biological research organization, the EMBL–European Bioinformatics Institute (EBI), part of the European Molecular Biology Laboratory. The EBI asked NBBJ to design a new east wing that would increase their capacity and, as the design team explains, provide staff with an inspiring and healthy work environment to carry out a critical scientific mission.

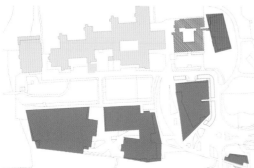

WELLCOME TRUST GENOME CAMPUS

- Wellcome Trust Sanger Institute (existing)
- Wellcome Trust Sanger Institute Expansion (NBBJ)
- EBI (existing)
- EBI Expansion (NBBJ)

The ongoing work of the Sanger Institute and other organizations like it generates an enormous amount of biological data, and the EBI is one of the few places in the world with the resources and expertise to collect and curate certain types of biological information, while also making it accessible to scientists around the world. The EBI's website gets an average two million hits a day. To maintain that essential service and continue research and training in bioinformatics, the EBI needed additional facilities.

The campus' rural setting was a source of inspiration for the Sanger Institute and became one for EBI too. Our design concept was a "building in a garden," a place that would provide bioinformaticists the space and technology they need for their intense, heads-down work, while opening up their workplace to the surrounding landscape.

We designed a new addition with flexible workspaces, a training suite, and social areas to encourage interaction among staff and external collaborators. We connected the new addition and the existing facilities with a glass corridor running through a terraced garden. The idea was to make a welcoming place for staff to gather and talk. East of the building is a forest, so we glazed the east façade, floor to ceiling, to maximize views and give staff the sense of working in nature. All the windows in the building can be opened, and a veil of finely perforated copper mesh provides sun shading and privacy. The project's use of passive low-energy strategies and its sensitivity to its rural and historic context earned it a BREEAM Excellent environmental rating.

BRUCE NEPP, PRINCIPAL, NBBJ

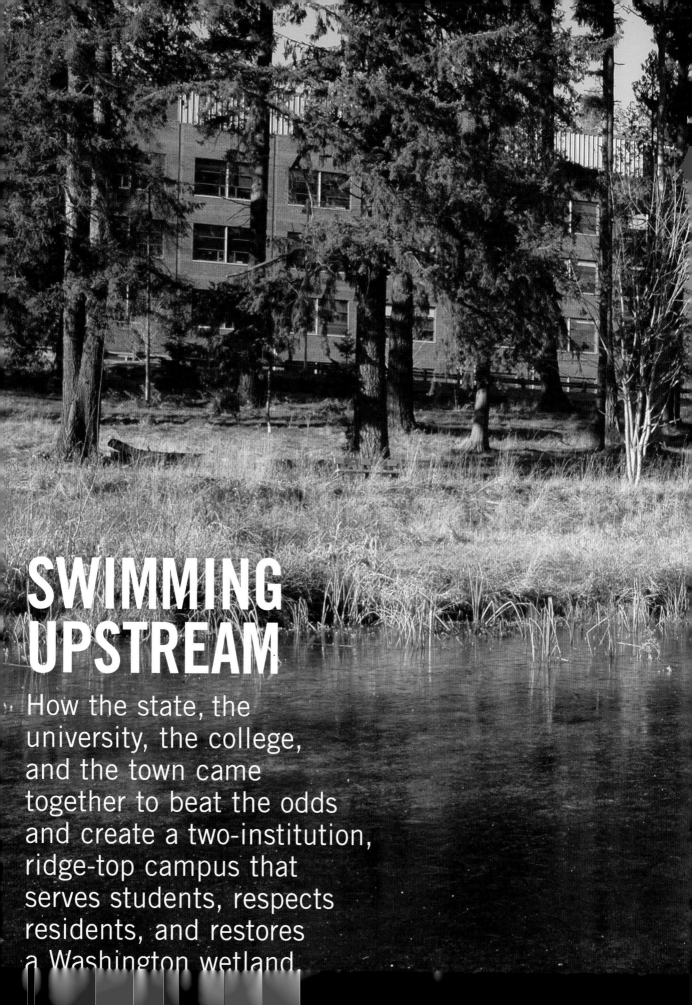

SWIMMING UPSTREAM

How the state, the university, the college, and the town came together to beat the odds and create a two-institution, ridge-top campus that serves students, respects residents, and restores a Washington wetland.

THE GOAL OF THE PROJECT IS TO PROVIDE A QUALITY LEARNING ENVIRONMENT IN A MANNER THAT MAXIMIZES RESTORATION AND PROTECTION OF THE ENVIRONMENT.

These were the areas where it looked as though the population of people of college and university age was going to be occurring? Right. You have to understand some background on this. The initial site for University of Washington Bothell was an area called Wellington Hills, but it was determined that that site couldn't be used, even though it had been bought, because it was outside the growth limit boundary.

At the same time we found out that the community colleges were seeking money to plan a new community college in that area, and one of the pieces of guidance we got from key state legislative members was that there was no way two campuses were going to be built within five miles of each other at the same time.

There are obvious distinctions between a community college and a university— one grants diplomas, the other degrees. Beyond that, how would you describe the differences in terms of their approach to education and the people they serve? In the community colleges you have some people who aren't interested in a baccalaureate-level education. Some need basic education, some need technical training. But you do have those who want to get their first two years at a community college and then transfer to a four-year institution.

The big difference between a baccalaureate institution and a community college is that the community colleges have what's called an "Open Door Policy," and essentially anyone can attend a community college. The baccalaureate institution, and this includes University of Washington, has admission standards. This underlay a lot of the tension we went through trying to get the University of Washington to support the notion of co-location with a community college. They were initially reluctant to do that.

What kind of university is the University of Washington? It's a research institution, Carnegie Class One—like Berkeley or UCLA. It receives more grant money than any other research university in the country. It's major. There are 35,000 students. The main campus in Seattle is like a city in itself.

Were they responding to this idea of having to share a campus with someone else in much the same way that any university would? Yes. I went to different parts of the country and talked to people who had tried co-location. There's typically some resistance from the four-year institutions. It gets into values and institutional culture and things like that. The prior administration at the UW was opposed to the idea. The Board of Regents was opposed. But over time, I think once they started to see the potential of the campus, things turned around.

The other problem that we were addressing was the site itself. It has some significant environmental issues. That was a major challenge being addressed at the same time that we were trying to get the two institutions to be willing partners.

Describe the site, and tell me a bit about why it was selected. It was selected because of its location. It's right off Highway 405. It's 130-some acres, but of that, about 55 acres are wetlands. We had to do a lot of analysis to make sure that the

PROJECT PROFILE

In the 1990s, Washington State's Higher Education Coordinating Board (HECB) identified a need for two new higher education institutions in the growing exurbia of Seattle—cities like Bellevue, Redmond, Bothell, and Woodinville.

The University of Washington (UW) and the State Board for Community and Technical Colleges (SBCTC) began separate searches, but after UW encountered obstacles in finding appropriate sites, the HECB recommended that the two entities share a campus.

The Truly Farm site in Bothell was selected to be the combined home of a branch campus of the University of Washington for upper division undergraduate and graduate students, and a newly created community college, Cascadia Community College.

In addition to co-locating the schools, the project included the largest wetlands restoration project ever undertaken in the State of Washington. The National Wildlife Federation gave the project high honors, and in 2008 Forbes Magazine listed the campus among the U.S.'s top-10 green college campuses.

The two schools have separate faculties, classrooms, and labor-atories but share a library, bookstore, parking, and food service.

Combining two institutes on one campus is expected to yield life-cycle cost savings of 10 percent over the 25-year planning horizon. Design and construction methods yielded an additional $6.5 million return to the state's coffers.

Both schools have seen significant increases in student enroll-ment. In 2008, UW Bothell saw a 21 percent increase and Cascadia Community College saw a 12 percent increase in student enrollment from Fall 2007.

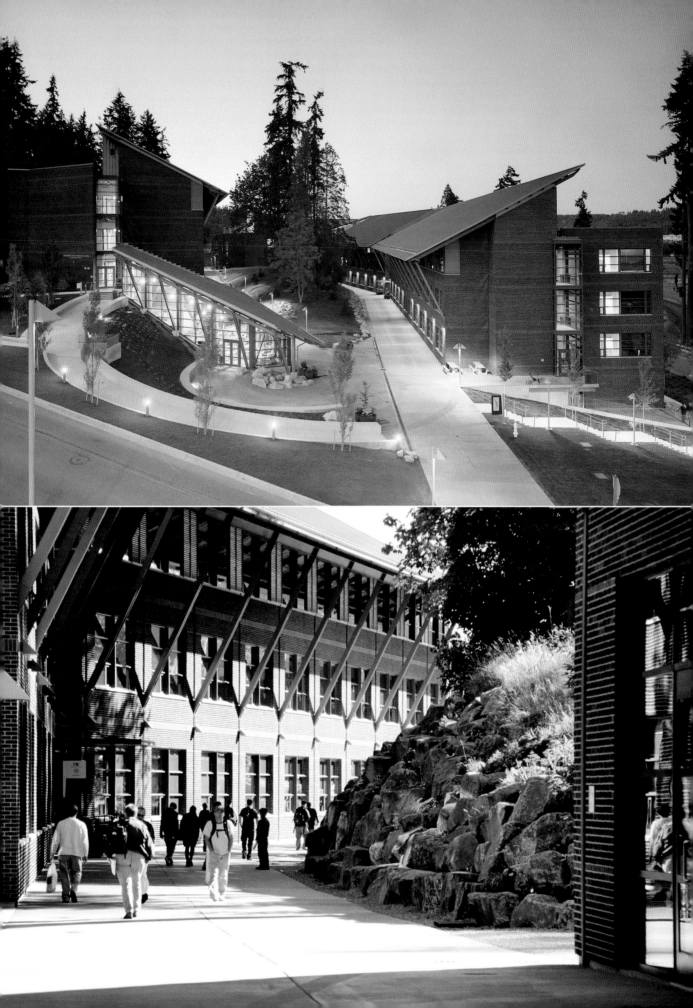

buildable area of the site could accommodate 10,000 students, because that was the build-out that we intended to have for the campus.

In this state, as in others, getting a permit to work on a wetland area is extremely difficult. It's administered by the Army Corps of Engineers. There was likelihood that we wouldn't get it from them. So we went through a number of activities to demonstrate to the Corps that technically and physically what we were going to do was worthwhile.

There was a creek that used to meander through the property years and years ago. It was moved to become a log flume.

This would have been, what, a century or so ago? Yes. Our plan was to move the creek back to its original area and then that would reduce the flooding that occurred on the site.

We eventually got the permit. A lot of that dealt with support from the community that had initially been opposed to the development of the site. Before we got involved with examining this site and potentially buying it, the owner had submitted plans to develop a regional shopping mall, and he was sued by the Washington Environmental Council, two other environmental groups, and the City of Bothell over his intent to fill the wetland.

When we got involved, that litigation was still underway. So we set up what was called a Site Development Advisory Committee and brought to the table the people who, a month before that, had literally been suing each other.

I also included representatives from the tribes and representatives from the Department of Ecology and Department of Transportation to work with us and develop a site plan that was acceptable to all the parties.

We'd meet monthly in the late afternoon or early evening down at NBBJ. We'd have a meal and sit and look at drawings and talk about concepts. The meal was important because, basically, if people will sit down and eat with each other, they're going to work out their problems. And they'd better have good food, too. There's a great Italian restaurant right behind NBBJ's building and they would cater the meals. It was great. If you can get people to commune, then they don't fear each other.

And it worked. I can remember when Bill Sanford [of NBBJ] and I went to get the final permit approval from the City of Bothell, the hearing examiner—who's like an administrative judge overseeing testimony—stated at the end, when he presented his findings, that this was the first time he'd ever seen a project that had no opposition. When you think about that in the context of the magnitude of this project and the environmental issues that were present at the site, that was a pretty rewarding statement.

You think you were able to accomplish that because of this process that you went through? Oh, definitely.

We also did a lot of external things to demonstrate that the community was behind this. We held countless community forums in the area where people could come and see how the campus would look. Lots of media. We would routinely brief key legislators. We'd do that both in Olympia and up at the NBBJ [Seattle] office.

Clearly you were a champion of that. Why were you convinced it could be a good thing? It was going to have to be. Once we had had to rule out Wellington Hills because you couldn't build there, this site was it.

So you had to make lemonade out of lemons? Yes. We needed a campus up there. There are very few developable sites in the area. So it was imperative that we figure out a way to succeed in acquiring the property and developing it for the campus.

You had very few precedents to look at, correct? Had this not been done very successfully elsewhere in the country? No. Many, many potential projects don't go forward because people can't get the wetlands permit, and a key element of the project was restoring the wetlands. And nothing in the country had ever, and to this day has ever, been done of that magnitude. Typically a project might have half an acre of a wetland that you have to mitigate. In other words, if you build on that, you've somehow got to go and acquire some other property to preserve the wetland. This was up to 60 acres.

So you had not one, but two precedent-setting opportunities, or challenges, depending on which way you look at it: this very large wetland restoration, and the bringing together of a college and a university in a co-location. Yes. In fact when I wrote the project plan and put out the Request for Proposals, I had worked through in my mind what the goal of this project was, and it was two things, but I didn't want to separate them because I didn't want to get into, "Is the first one more important than the second?" So I wrote something to the effect that the goal of the project is to provide a quality learning environment in a manner that maximizes restoration and protection of the environment. Those aren't the exact words, but it was a way to recognize both things we were trying to do.

Let's get back to the point at which you had everything in place except for the agreement of the University of Washington. How did you ultimately get that? Well, there was a change in university administration, a new president, and I think that was instrumental. I think the public support was instrumental. And once the actual people who would be working at the campus were getting together and doing what's called the programming phase, then that really helped. Because they could see each other, and see that they weren't, you know, Martians.

CHANGE DESIGN
TOOL IN ACTION

SITE SEE

Change is not a one-size-fits-all proposition, and the tools NBBJ has developed to help accomplish it recognize that. "Site See" is a tool that searches for the unique physical and experiential characteristics of a site. On this project, the contextual thinking it provoked led to a better environment for everyone.

SEE PAGE 184 FOR MORE INFORMATION ABOUT THIS TOOL.

THE RIDGE REVELATION

For about three or four years the design team was operating with an understanding that the site was an upper table and a lower shelf. The town of Bothell sat on the higher level, the freeway interchange was on the lower level, and the difference between the bottom and the top was a very distinct slope. Usually, steep slopes are the delicate and fragile parts of a landscape; you get erosion. So, generally, you don't touch the slopes. That's what was operating here.

All of the development options were occurring on the top level. The problem was that it displaced the conifers, a little remnant of forest that the community was very sensitive about. But if the development went below the slope, it would interrupt the restoration of a stream. So the design team was betwixt and between. Nothing worked up above, nothing worked down below, and the development options began to thin out until there was discouragement.

So NBBJ was withdrawn and another architectural firm began work on the project. They too zeroed out, because they too protected the slope. They went to the bottom land and displaced the wetlands. Within a year the project went back to NBBJ.

You can get fixed on an idea, and keep working on options for it. NBBJ had had 10 different campus plans for the upper level. And once you're that deep into an assumption, it's hard to back up. Now, the abrupt changes of situation—another architect coming in, then receiving the project back—didn't feel good. But that's sometimes when freshness comes and the available answers start showing up.

And, indeed, that's when there was a revelation, this beautiful moment when the problem became the solution. The design team said, "What if this slope could be replaced? Put in a new slope,

and let that be the campus. Protect the top, protect the bottom, and feed the two institutions from end to end along the slope." Suddenly everything began to unfold. At one end of the slope was a smaller piece of property and at the other was a larger piece of property, so the University of Washington could take the heavy end and have its identity, and Cascadia, the smaller school, could take the smaller end and have its identity. We could save most of the conifers and restore the stream.

Most effective designers, whether architects or engineers or landscape architects, believe the same thing: if

you are really creative with understanding the issues and the problems and the nature of a place, you will find the answer; it's usually inherent in the circumstances at hand. You don't have to invent the answer, you don't have to bring it in from Italy or somewhere else in the world; it's there. It's a question of uncovering it.

BILL JOHNSON, NBBJ

AT THE FINAL HEARING THEY SAID THIS IS A GOOD THING FOR THE ENVIRONMENT, A GOOD THING FOR THE CITY, AND A GOOD THING FOR THE STUDENTS.

What was NBBJ's role throughout this process? They were my right arm. They and their sub-consultants. They were planning in an architectural development sense, but they were also managing all these different forces with me.

It certainly sounds like a marshalling of forces was one of the real challenges here. Yes. We opened a storefront office in this little village of Bothell, and NBBJ would staff it four days a week, and we'd have drawings up and cookies, coffee, and invite people off the street in. We had a newsletter that went out quarterly, and it would talk about the project, where we were. We had a very long mailing list.

We had these external strategies and I think when the administration changed at the university and the actual faculty members sat down to do the programming of the spaces with the community college, I think that was key. It was getting to that point that was a little rocky at times. There were many times when this project could have died. Many times.

What was the history up to that point of the concept of co-located higher education institutions? Some had worked across the country, some had been dissolved, some were still operating but not very well, and there were a few success stories. One of the things we did to get ourselves educated, but also to help the UW to see that it wasn't going to hurt, was to hold a symposium. We brought in people—I believe it was from five different states, including Hawaii, Texas, Florida, and Kentucky—people who were at successful and unsuccessful co-location sites. It was a two- or three-day conference, and each of those parties got up and went over how they had approached co-location, what went well, and what failed.

What came out of that? Lessons learned. One that comes to mind immediately was the need for the two institutions to have a joint operating agreement that would clarify the respective roles and document their respective rights. That came from one of the states that made a presentation at our symposium. That was a key thing that the two institutions subsequently adopted, and it's still in force.

I can imagine that both institutions would have very much wanted to ensure that they had their own identity on this campus. Right. Every time we would meet with community members, we would make sure that the university and Cascadia people were there and we would always emphasize that this campus was going to preserve the identity and promote the identity of the two different institutions. We got that message out very clearly.

Long before the campus was built, when NBBJ prepared the renderings of what it would look like, it was a very student-oriented space. The circulation patterns through and around the buildings and how it would blend in with the hillside and the trees. I think when people started to look at what this place was going to look like, they said, "Hmm. That might not be too bad!"

According to an article I read about the opening of the co-located campus, there was still talk that the differences between the university and the college—

including funding, salary levels, and teaching loads—would be difficult, if not impossible to surmount. **What has happened since then?** I know people were talking about that, but that differential is going to exist between any community college and any four-year institution. That was my argument. Those differences have nothing to do with co-location. Co-location doesn't cause that.

Has being on the same campus started to subdue some of that sense of difference? I believe so, yes. Norm Rose, University of Washington's dean, who's now retired, was pretty opposed to the co-location initially, and he hated the site. I remember after construction started, he called me one day and he said, "You know, I've got to tell you, I had this whole thing wrong. I didn't understand the potential that the wetlands restoration would provide to the students."

Because I had said, "Look, you're going to have the largest restored wetlands in the country, and one program that's very big at the UW is Environmental Sciences." When he saw that they could incorporate that resource, the wetlands, into an academic program, he was excited.

Can we talk a bit more about that? How is the campus, now that it's been open for several years, serving the people who you initially set out to serve back in the early '90s? It's doing great. Both the institutions offer good programs. The first phase, as students filled it up, has actually exceeded the enrollment plans. The interest side is there. The demand to attend there exists. And the output is there. They're graduating students with AA degrees and baccalaureate-level degrees. And that's what we wanted.

And what do you hear from the community that was initially so opposed to this site being used? Well, every member of the Advisory Group, at the final hearing—when we had a final hearing on the Environmental Impact Statement—got up and supported the project. Every single one. They said that it was a good thing for the environment, that it was a good thing for the City of Bothell, and that it was a good thing for the students.

Do you get a sense of what it means for the students of both institutions to be sharing with each other? I think for the community college students, those who don't immediately have a plan to get a bachelor's degree, there are some who don't go further because they don't believe they'd be able to succeed. My theory was that they could see other people like themselves, enrolled as juniors at the University of Washington, succeeding, and just by association, by talking with them, be encouraged. I don't have any measure that that happened, but I think it did.

Since the national consensus initially was that a co-location of a community college and a university either shouldn't or couldn't be done, what kind of interest have you been fielding in the project? I think there have been three different doctoral students who did dissertations on it. All kinds of other articles have been written about it. It got a national award for planning from an international education planning group. There have been a lot of inquiries as to how it got done.

What do you tell people who call to inquire? People from other states who want to try to do this themselves? The key thing is to get the goal and stay focused on the goal, and keep that in front of you and all the people who you're going to have to work with.

JUSTICE SERVED

Seattle's U.S. District Court made a federal case out of stage sets and sightlines, libraries and lily ponds in order to build a courthouse that inspires awe, comfort, and judicial efficiency.

BRUCE RIFKIN

DISTRICT COURT EXECUTIVE, UNITED STATES DISTRICT COURT, WESTERN
DISTRICT OF WASHINGTON

For more than 20 years, Bruce Rifkin has served as District Court Executive/Clerk
of Court for the United States District Court for the Western District of Washington.
He was appointed as Deputy Trial Court Administrator in Dade County Florida
[Miami] and Attorney/Advisor for the Administrative Office of the United States
Courts prior to moving to the Western District of Washington. He has held
positions as chair of the Ninth Circuit Clerks Liaison Committee and national
representative to the District Clerks Advisory Group. In 1998, he received the
Directors Award for Outstanding Leadership, which is awarded nationally to one
or two individuals in recognition of contributions to the federal judiciary. The
award was given for the development of a comprehensive training program for
federal judges and senior managers participating in the planning, design, and
construction of new courthouses.

**Let's start by talking about traditional federal courthouses as they were first
built, 200 years ago, in cities across America. What were those buildings
supposed to say to Americans?** In the early days they were the center of the
community, on the town square. They were often the most solemn, formal
structure, and even as cities began to grow in the 18th, 19th, and early 20th
centuries, they were often the most formidable structure in town.

**"Formidable" implies something that people would approach with a certain
amount of awe.** Awe, and solemnity. The old courthouses mirrored classical
architectural treatment; they had columns and details you didn't see in other
buildings. From one town to the next, you could recognize the courthouse
without having to read what was on the mantel because it was always the most
prominent civic building.

And what was Seattle's old federal courthouse like? The tradition that I'm talking about started on the east coast. By contrast, we're a relatively new part of the
country. Our old courthouse was constructed in the 1930s and, although people
don't like to acknowledge this, it wasn't much of a building. It was part of the
New Deal construction approach, where a government architect said, "This is
what courthouses are going to look like: a rectangular box." The courthouse in
Los Angeles was built at the same time and it looks very similar, just larger.

WE WANTED THIS TO BE AN INVITING BUILDING AND PLAZA, MORE INVITING THAN ANY OTHER SITE IN THE CITY.

How did it function for you, in your role as chief clerk? I'm in my 27th year here, and from my perspective, the old courthouse was not really very functional. Here's an example. Since the courthouse was first built, it's become increasingly, critically important to segregate judges and prisoners, for security reasons. In the old building there was no segregation. The prisoners went down the hallways, and even into the elevators, with the judges.

And it was not a very flexible structure with respect to 21st century technology. In the old days, at best you had a phone line. Now if you needed to cable the building it was a nightmare. It had cement floors two-and-a-half-feet thick. It also had large pillars that didn't make for an atmosphere very conducive to working.

In courthouses of the same age across the country, in the 1980s, the General Services Administration (GSA) inaugurated a very ambitious program to build new courthouses. What was the goal of that federal program? The GSA is the developer for the federal government. Prior to the 1980s it hadn't built a new courthouse in something like 20 years. What happened during that time is the judiciary grew without gaining any additional facilities. You can't move a trial court. You can't move prisoners into a private office building. So the courthouse had to displace everybody that it could. By the time we had a new building, the bankruptcy court, the probation office, the pre-trial office, the United States Attorney were all in leased spaces.

At the same time, the GSA, through new leadership, created the program of design excellence. Our demand hit their program. One of the first courthouses that came to fruition was in Boston. The judges there wanted an extraordinary building to meet the judiciary's needs—and that's exactly what the GSA wanted through its design excellence program.

That program has since given the country many new courthouses that have become icons for the cities they're in. But one of the design precepts for the Seattle courthouse was that the icon element, design excellence, be balanced with functional performance. Why was the latter given equal importance in that equation? By the time we started to think about our new building, we could point to courthouses that had already been constructed—extraordinary icons, wonderful buildings—where a commitment to the excellence of what was inside, to the performance of the building, had, sometimes, been lost. I don't think it was lost out of ill will. It was because performance hadn't been made an absolutely committed goal of the architecture.

And we saw that. It's not a matter of being critical, but we would go into those buildings, on tours, and say, "My God, what an unbelievable piece of architecture, but man, it doesn't work!" At least in our view. And I haven't met a colleague yet who disagrees. There's always compromise, but it was our impression that functionality had not been given—I like the way you put it—equal importance.

At the same time that you had to balance iconic significance and functionality, within the functionality you had a balance as well. The building has to function for both the justice system and for the public. What was it that you wanted the building to say to and do for the American public? The challenge was to portray

PROJECT PROFILE

Created as the outgrowth of the Hoover Commission in 1949, the General Services Administration (GSA) secures the buildings, products, services, technology, and other workplace essentials that federal agencies need.

The GSA's public building service is the largest commercial real estate organization in the United States. It provides 34.5 million square feet (3.2 million square meters) of workspace for more than one million federal employees in 2,000 American communities.

In the 1990s, the GSA undertook the largest courthouse construction program in more than 50 years. The U.S. courthouse in downtown Seattle is one of the projects recently completed as part of the GSA's Design and Construction Excellence Program. Accommodating 500 employees, it triples the space of the courthouse it replaces, which was built in 1938.

The new 23-story, 615,000-square-foot (57,135-square-meter) federal courthouse encompasses a full city block in downtown Seattle. The structure has three primary components: a courtroom tower, judicial chambers, and office bar.

It houses the U.S. district court, U.S. bankruptcy court, United States Attorney, and other court-related agencies.

It includes 13 district courtrooms, five bankruptcy courtrooms, and 22 judicial chambers suites.

The courthouse is the nation's first to include universally sized district and magistrate courtrooms, reducing the number of total courtrooms needed. Courtrooms and judicial libraries are shared, with each courtroom floor containing three judicial chambers adjacent to two courtrooms.

10X

MORE OUTDOOR SPACE

To create open plaza space, 18 courtrooms were stacked two per floor into a tower. By using this massing strategy, the additional outdoor space was 10 times larger than required by local zoning code.

the importance and publicness of the building, without making it a fortress. That was the goal. I'll refer back to the old building. We had had the only lawn in downtown Seattle. We had green all around us, in a city that really doesn't have that. Now, we weren't going to put a lawn around the new courthouse—that doesn't make sense in the 21st century—but it was very important to have room on the site. That idea impacted the blocking of the building and led to us having towers.

When it came to the plaza itself, we didn't want it hardscaped. At a lot of the new courthouses, the plaza tends to be very hard. We didn't want ours to feel like a cement platform. So we have a forest of birch trees; we have pathways of stepping-stones with grass growing between.

We wanted this to be an inviting building and plaza, more inviting than any other site in the city. We wanted people from the neighborhood, people just walking by, to come and sit.

So, really, quite the inverse of formidable. Yes. A place that is formal, but draws you in. And I do think it is both. The building has the formality; the plaza has the informality. When you sit in the plaza you feel this extraordinary, strong structure around you, but you sit on benches, under the trees. Just today, we had music in the plaza at lunch, and people came to sit, to listen and eat. We have water features with lily ponds. We use them as a security device, to separate the secure area from the public area. That means when you come up the steps into the portico, you can actually go into the building without being immediately met by security. We have a strong and impressive building, but at the same time an inviting plaza and an open portico.

In terms of how the building needed to function for the justice system, you alluded a little earlier to how the federal court is home to many agencies. How do their needs differ? The hardest tenants are the judges, their courtrooms and chambers. Most of the other tenants primarily need office space. I don't want to diminish the other tenants' needs, but they weren't as difficult to address as the judges'. Courthouses start with courtrooms. They're so complex that if you don't think through how you're going to meet those challenges, they may not work. So the goal was to try to create a kind of a tripartite building, where the first part was the courtrooms, the second was the judges' chambers adjacent to those courtrooms, and the third part was all the rest.

Early on, the judges were sent a questionnaire, as part of an effort called Enhanced Office Programming. What did it ask of you and your colleagues? There was a questionnaire and a set of interviews. NBBJ asked us to define what we do, how we operate, how we would like to operate. They asked us not to just accept what we did before as necessarily what we ought to be doing now. We were in a position to make changes if that would be beneficial. The process led to some very interesting changes from the way we had previously operated.

What changes were most significant? For the judges, I'll be specific. Each judge is entitled to a certain square footage that includes a reception area, a library, two offices—one for each of the law clerks—the judge's personal office, and a workroom/lunchroom combo.

When NBBJ did the Enhanced Office Programming, they asked about that configuration. What's good about it and what's bad? If you had the chance to change it, what would you do? What do you want from your space? And out of all that discussion, a couple of things came out. One, with the advent of electronic access to law books, the judges recognized that to build another library for each

THE GSA IS REDOING THE JUDICIARY DESIGN GUIDE AND CHOSE THIS BUILDING, OUT OF ALL OF THE FEDERAL COURTHOUSES, TO LOOK AT.

of them really didn't make any sense. The kinds of things that are not on-line tend to be specialty publications that certainly could be shared.

The other thing that came out of the discussion was this: our federal judges get the top law students in the world; they come in to work for law school credit. But you can't build space for these students because they're not in our design guide. The guide hasn't recognized that these people exist, yet they do. The answer can't just be, "Let's add to the square footage." You have to work within the space that's allowed.

We melded those two observations. One, that books are not so much less important, just less necessary, and two, that we need space for people who provide invaluable service to us but are not in the program. So, NBBJ came out from Enhanced Programming with a design that has three chambers on a floor sharing one central library. We reduced our collection of books by two-thirds—that's a huge savings in money. And the central library is a wonderful, two-story space with floor-to-ceiling glass and room for these beautiful carrels for the externs.

The plan was square-footage neutral but the judges ended up having space organized in a fashion that, if you walked through it with them, they would say they love. It gives them much more functionality than they had before, than they would have had if we had divided the space as authorized under the design guide. That was all a direct product of Enhanced Programming.

One other significant change involved my office, the clerk's office. In many courthouses, including ours, it's on the main floor. Usually, you walk into the grand public space, then go through a set of doors saying, "Clerk's Office" and end up in the transaction space—a big waiting area with a counter. I said, "I just don't like that." When I see a grand space, I want to interact with it directly. So, part of our design is that we have two grand spaces: a large portico and then a seven-story atrium. And my intake is part of that atrium. It goes to what I want the public to feel. I want them to realize that when they're thinking, "Oh, man, this is an extraordinary atrium, with a glass skylight seven stories up"—that extraordinary place is where they do their business.

When you were describing the outdoor public spaces, you talked a bit about security. Construction began pre-9/11, but the building was completed in the post-9/11 world, where security's even more of a major issue for everyone than it already was. We faced the security issues pre-9/11, but you're right, everyone is more conscious of it now. You know that we had somebody who tried to get in here with fake hand grenades, a couple of weeks ago [June 2005]; did you realize that?

Yes, let's talk about that. There was a violent incident at the courthouse where an armed man was shot and killed inside the lobby by security guards. How did the building function during that emergency? The building as a building, as a design, functioned the way we would hope it would function. The man was contained in the front by security, and that's all we could ask for. That's what we did ask for. I guess we could have made it even harder for him if we had done

what other courts did, which is to just put up a wall instead of using a water moat. And we will make some minimal changes to the water feature; we'll put in some wonderful architectural features so people can't shimmy along the little wall that we do have there. But I think everyone is quite satisfied that, even though we had the openness, it did provide the security. Any concerns we have post-incident have to do with our internal command and control. The building was fine.

You had a national workshop not long ago that brought judges from all over the country to Seattle, and they had an opportunity to see your new courthouse. What was the general response? A variety of groups have tracked through. In September [2004], right after we moved in, there was a national conference in Seattle of the United States District Court judges. Judges came from new and old courthouses all over the country, and we toured them through our building. I think it's a very handsome building, and they were struck by that. But—for me this is the most important—they looked at those choices that our judges made under the Enhanced Office Programming and said, "My God, that makes sense. What a functional place."

The GSA is redoing the judiciary's design guide right now, and this building was the one chosen, out of all of them, to look at, because although we designed it under the old design guide, we were the only place that could demonstrate how you can think through what you can do with space that might give you better solutions. NBBJ showed us better ways to use the space to meet our goals and objectives. And it is a beautiful building. We didn't sacrifice anything.

Judge John C. Coughenour is the Chief Judge of the Western District of Washington and is the past President of the Ninth Circuit District Judges Association. He has served as chair of the Ninth Circuit Jury Instructions and the Intracircuit Assignment Committees, and as chair of the Ninth Circuit Gender Bias Task Force. Judge Coughenour was born in Pittsburg, Kansas, and graduated from Kansas State College of Pittsburg in 1963. He received his Juris Doctor degree from the University of Iowa in 1966, where he was Order of the Coif and a member of the Board of Editors of the Iowa Law Review. He taught trial and appellate practice at the University of Washington School of Law from 1970 to 1973. Judge Coughenour was a partner at the Seattle law firm of Bogle and Gates when he was appointed to the United States District Court in 1981.

JOHN C. COUGHENOUR
UNITED STATES DISTRICT JUDGE, WESTERN DISTRICT OF WASHINGTON

Most of us get our ideas about justice from Hollywood, where a trial seems satisfying if there's lots of grandstanding and arm-waving. In real life, how do you measure the success of a trial? I think the ultimate measure is whether I'm satisfied, at the conclusion of the trial, that the right thing was done, that the jury came to the right verdict, or if it's without a jury that I was able to see facts that made me confident that I could rule one way or another and not do a lot of mischief. A lot of times, cases that get tried are tried because there are good arguments on both sides, and it's sometimes very difficult to cut through all of it and feel really comfortable that you've done the right thing.

If you think about it, some of the best final arguments you've seen in movies or on television are probably in the neighborhood of two to three minutes. The producer of a TV program or a movie can't afford to spend more time than that on one aspect of the story. Well, in the same case, if tried in a real courtroom, those arguments would take hours instead of minutes.

And that makes more demands on you and on the jury. Yes. Sometimes it causes the jury or the judge to lose interest—in the middle of the afternoon when it gets stuffy and late and everybody's tired and the lawyers are droning on about something nobody cares about. A lot of good trial lawyers say that after 20 minutes in an argument you're going to have to fight to keep the attention of the jury or the judge.

I teach a class in how to try lawsuits, and one of the things I draw analogies to is the making of a movie, the presentation of a play.

Courtrooms are sometimes referred to as theatrical spaces. Is that what you're alluding to? Yes, I am. A movie or a play or a trial. They're all exercises in communication.

Over the course of your career you've worked in courthouses across the country. What are some of the ways that the physical space of a courtroom can help or hinder that communication? The most important thing, in my mind, is that when somebody walks into a federal courtroom they should have an immediate impression, subconsciously if not consciously, that this is an important place, that something extraordinary is about to happen here, that this isn't just another meeting room.

In some of our county courthouses, particularly in metropolitan areas, the counties have been so besieged by budget problems that whenever they look for places to save money the courts end up with short shrift. And, as a consequence, in a lot of our county courts, the feeling you get when you walk into the courtroom is this is a scruffy, not very clean place where dirty business is done.

The federal courts, on the other hand, have been very successful in persuading Congress that it's extremely important that our courthouses and our courtrooms be a statement of federal presence in the community, and that when people walk into the courtroom they realize that this is a significant and very important place.

There are some classic examples around the country of courtrooms in older buildings that are ornate and exquisite places—carved walnut and marble and the like—but you just can't afford to do that sort of thing anymore. It's hard for architects now to design a courtroom that accomplishes everything that we want to accomplish. NBBJ spent a lot of time with us talking about these things.

Have the demands that the justice system places on a courtroom changed over the course of time? No, not really. Going back to the thought I mentioned earlier, it really is an exercise in communication and, by and large, we still try cases the way

WHEN YOU WALK INTO A FEDERAL COURTROOM, YOU SHOULD HAVE AN IMMEDIATE IMPRESSION THAT SOMETHING EXTRAORDINARY IS GOING TO HAPPEN HERE.

Abe Lincoln did, with a lawyer standing up in front of a jury or a judge and talking to them and communicating with them.

There are a few things that have changed—and for the better. Electronic document handling has sped up document-intensive cases, and the electronic document-handling system we have in this building is state-of-the-art; it helps us move trials along faster. Real-time court reporting is another example of something that is a little different since I started practicing. Now we get a transcript on the computer screen a few seconds after the actual words are spoken. And the ability of lawyers to access the Internet from counsel table in the courtroom and do legal research right from counsel table with their computers is something else that is different. We did some of that in our old building and it required jackhammering concrete floors to create tunnels for cable. This new building has a cable vault below the floor so that it's a lot easier to make modifications as technology changes.

The other thing that has been a significant improvement is the ability to put monitors in the jury box for the jurors to see documents up close. For example, if a witness is testifying about a particular document, and a lawyer is focusing the witness's attention on a particular sentence in the document, the document is on a monitor right in front of the jurors while it is also in front of the witness and the lawyer and the judge, and then the lawyer can highlight the sentence and the yellow highlight comes up on the monitor.

So the jury's focus is centered on what everybody's talking about, whereas before you either had to use an overhead projector, which was clumsy and often very difficult to locate in the courtroom so everybody could see it.

Another area where technology has been successful is sometimes we have to read testimony, from depositions or the like. The old approach was to have somebody on the witness stand who was reading the answers and the lawyer reads the questions and everybody goes to sleep.

Now, they do that but at the same time the transcript is scrolling down the screen on the monitors with a highlight that is following where the witness is in the reading, so that the jury and the judge and everybody else is on the same page, and it's a little more effective.

You mentioned that NBBJ spent a lot of time getting to know you and your needs. You, along with a number of your colleagues, were asked to fill out a questionnaire about those needs, and the design team responded to it by showing you images. They called it a "Visual Design Dialogue." What struck you as the most important questions and images about courtrooms? I was very impressed with that whole process. At first I thought that I had more important things to do, but as I watched the architects change their view of things based upon what we said to them, I realized that we were really having a significant impact on what the final product would be.

For example, a number of us emphasized that not just the courtroom itself, but the courthouse too ought to have a feeling that this is not just another office building. This is a statement of federal presence in the community. And one of the architects laughingly said, "Be careful when you tell an architect to build a monument!"

But to a certain degree that's what we were saying, that this is a building that is being built for a hundred years and should have some classic grandeur about it. One of the judges who was in town for our recent committee meeting had never seen our building and she didn't know where the courthouse was, she just knew the general direction. She was staying at the Grand Hyatt and she said as she came down 7th Avenue and approached Stewart, she looked across the street and said to herself, "That's it." And that's exactly what we were trying to accomplish.

The design process ended up in a full-scale mock-up that you could walk around in. What was that experience like, and what did you learn from it? One of the biggest problems in designing courtrooms is always line of sight. Going back to my original concept that a trial is an exercise in communication, you have communication between lawyer and judge, you have communication between lawyer and witness, you have communication between witness and judge, communication between lawyer and jury, communication between witness and jury, and judge and jury, communication between jury and monitors. All of these lines of sight and communication are critical to a trial because the interplay between the judge and the lawyers is important, the interplay between the lawyers and the jury is important, the interplay between the witness and the lawyer, the witness and the jury, the witness and the judge are all important.

And you're talking about communication not just on a verbal level? Yes, exactly. The judge, the jury, the lawyers, everybody needs to watch the demeanor of the witness. For example, a major portion of credibility determination is based upon body language: does the witness appear to be nervous, is the witness sweating, is the witness stammering? All these things help one make a decision as to whether somebody's blowing smoke in your face or not.

And in a non-jury trial in particular you need a very effective line of sight between judge and lawyer, because that's a source of a tremendous amount of information that the judge uses to make a decision about the case. Well, you can't modify the courtroom every time you have a change in whether it's jury or non-jury, or you have a motion argument where there's not even a witness involved. All of this has to be anticipated in setting up the courtroom. And every judge has his or her own point of view of what's important in terms of setup. So we spent a lot of time in the mock-up talking about individual preferences. By the time the mock-up exercise was over, we had what everybody was satisfied was going to be the final design.

And in the end what you got was very close to the mock-up? Yes, it was.

You also used the mock-up to look at the materials and finishes. Why was that something to test drive? I suppose I'm as much to blame for that as anybody, because one of the things that I always felt set our old courthouse apart from just another office building was the beautiful walnut-finish woodwork in the chambers and in the courtrooms. So from the very beginning I was harping on paying attention to the quality of the millwork. Part of that was because I had tried a long case over in Helena, Montana, in a courtroom in a courthouse that was built without a whole lot of judge input; it was just a GSA project that nobody paid a whole lot of attention to and the millwork in that thing was an abomination. It looked like plywood that had had stain slapped on it.

And if you're trying to communicate the gravity of this occasion... It's awfully hard to do in a place where the workmanship is as shoddy as it was in that building. And, you know, the finishing didn't turn out to be as much of a problem as

CHANGE DESIGN
TOOL IN ACTION

SPEAK THE RIGHT LANGUAGE

Change happens as a result of new understandings. To ensure that everyone on the project team understands the connection between their enterprise and their design, NBBJ uses a simple but powerful tool called "Speak the Right Language." On the Seattle U.S. District Court, this tool drove us to find a common language that was comfortable for the client and productive for the project.

SEE PAGE 200 FOR MORE INFORMATION ABOUT THIS TOOL.

VISUAL DESIGN DIALOGUE

We put together a questionnaire and asked the federal judges to fill it out. In a way, that was presumptuous of us, but they were willing to engage the case for the questionnaire: you live in the written world, the world of precedents, so the design team is going to meet you in your world with words and thoughts. The team took the judges' responses and associated with those answers a range of visual imagery, creating what's called a "Visual Design Dialogue." This then became a bridge from the written world to the visual world of design. On the strength of these images, the design team and the judges established a common ground and common reference points.

The questionnaire was intentionally provocative. One of the questions dealt with classicism in architecture. The design team quickly moved the judges from preconceived ideas about the building to thinking "it's the idea of a portico that matters, not that it has the right order of columns." The Visual Design Dialogue showed Dulles Airport and its colonnade—its clear organization and the verticality of the front façade is evocative of the federal presence in Washington D.C. and yet it's a modern interpretation.

Throughout the judicial system there are many stories of architects and judges gone astray and yet here was a relationship built on the substance of content and on the sharing of ideas and thinking.

STEVE McCONNELL, PARTNER, NBBJ

I thought it would be. The GSA was in sync with what I was saying, and the architects were careful. This is an area where you don't have to spend a lot of extra money to get good quality stuff, you just have to pay attention to the specifications. I was delighted with the quality of the millwork and the finishing that was done.

At the start of this conversation you talked about measuring the success of a trial in terms of communication. How do you see the new courtrooms working in that regard? They work very well. There are a couple of fundamentals that are important in a courtroom. One is good lighting. The architects did a very good job of paying a lot of attention to the quality of the lighting. In other courtrooms I've been in around the country, and even in our old building, the light was not as good in some places as it was in other places; it was spotty. And I've been in new courtrooms where you'll see people bringing in supplemental lights, desk lamps and the like, because the overhead lighting is not good, or it has glare. But the lighting in these rooms is very nice.

And a large amount of it is daylight. Why is that important? It makes a difference in terms of people getting tired. With all the visual demands that are placed upon jurors and judges, it's important to have natural light. We had plenty of natural light in the old building, but here the architects did a nice job of positioning the windows. First of all, they're behind the jurors so that the jurors aren't looking into bright light; it comes over their shoulders into the courtroom. And secondly, the windows are high enough and the baffles are situated such that your attention isn't drawn outside, away from the courtroom, and yet you still have the

THE COURTHOUSE OUGHT TO HAVE A FEELING THAT THIS IS NOT JUST ANOTHER OFFICE BUILDING. THIS IS A STATEMENT OF FEDERAL PRESENCE IN THE COMMUNITY.

natural light coming into the courtroom. In the old building you had to keep the drapes drawn to keep jurors from looking out at the trees or seeing whether it's raining. Here we don't have that problem.

The other thing that's extremely important in a courtroom is acoustics, again as a communication exercise, and the acoustics in the old building were not that good. We had terrible problems with the PA systems. They were antiquated, and the wiring was bad. The electronic communication system in this building is just superb.

Another thing that has surprised me a little was I had a big case, a criminal case, involving a total of about 12 defendants, and each of them had at least one lawyer, so you've got 24 to 30 defendants and lawyers, and then a team of lawyers for the government. Ideally the courtroom would have been half again as big as it was, but I was surprised at how well we were able to handle that many people. In the old courtroom it would have been a real hassle. Here, the architects custom-built counsel tables that are units. You can add more units and not change the appearance of the tables.

Each of the things you're describing—each one on its own is a subtle thing, a small thing. and yet what you're describing is a place where every small thing that happens has an impact. Well, it should, if it's being done the way it's supposed to be done.

I can remember in college being told that one of the signature characteristics of Greek tragedy is that every word contributes to the central theme. That ought to be true of a trial if it's being well-tried. A tremendous amount of stuff happens in a very short period of time, stuff that somebody's going to be living with, in some cases, for decades, and so what happens there is extremely important. Whether you have a good view of the witness and can easily watch the witness's facial expressions and body language as the testimony's going on, and whether it's easy for the jury to move their focus from the witness to the lawyer. If it requires them to turn their entire body around they won't do it, and yet it's important for them to be able to watch both of these things easily, and that's hard to accomplish in most courtrooms. It's all a compromise, but you get it as good as you can. You can't get it perfect and accomplish all these things because some of them are exclusive to others.

But when you get a balance of those little things, justice works. Well, it works better.

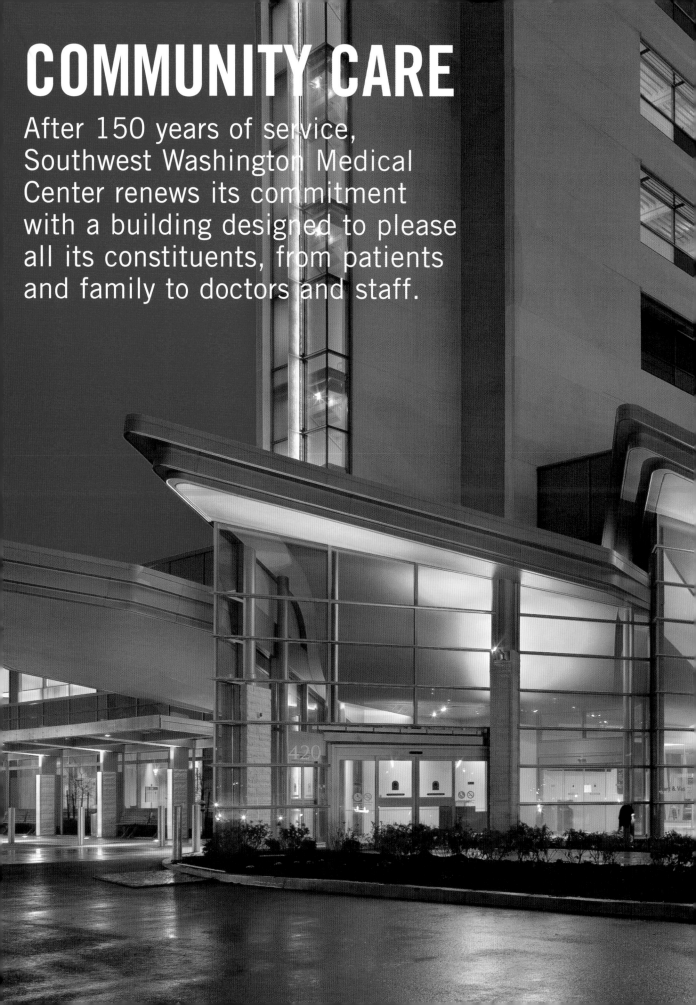

COMMUNITY CARE

After 150 years of service, Southwest Washington Medical Center renews its commitment with a building designed to please all its constituents, from patients and family to doctors and staff.

JOSEPH KORTUM
PRESIDENT AND CEO, SOUTHWEST WASHINGTON MEDICAL CENTER

Joseph Kortum serves as President and Chief Executive Officer of both the Southwest Washington Health System and the Southwest Washington Medical Center (SWMC). Before joining SWMC in 2003, he served as President and CEO of the Northern Arizona Healthcare System, Flagstaff, Arizona, and was the Chief Operating Officer of Mercy Medical Center in Redding, California. Kortum holds a Master's in Hospital and Healthcare Administration from St. Louis University and is a Fellow of the American College of Healthcare Executives. He is also a member of the governing boards for the Washington State Hospital Association, Voluntary Hospitals of America West Coast, Chair of Southwest Washington Hospital Council and the Advisory Board for Washington State University, Vancouver, and was formerly the Chairman of the Arizona Hospital Association.

Shortly after you became CEO of Southwest Washington Medical Center, you got involved in the project to build a new facility. What were your priorities, as a newcomer to Southwest, for the development of the campus? My biggest concern when I first arrived here was the fact that this campus was decades old, and multiple little projects over that time had resulted in something of a disjointed campus, from a functional standpoint. So I was motivated to start a course that would create a more intelligent juxtaposition of services. We realized that you don't do that overnight, that it would take decades, but that we had to begin planning a transformation that would get us away from a campus that looked like it had been designed by committee to one that fit together. We wanted to create an impression. I've always felt that a patient, by the time they hit the front door of a hospital, has already drawn conclusions about the quality of care they're going to get based on the visual experience of a facility. I think people can relate to this. When you're house shopping, the first time a real estate agent drives you up to a house, you have an opinion about it. Before you've even seen the inside, the kitchen or the living room, you're going to be favorably inclined or not, based on the experience you have driving up to the building.

The way you're describing it, there's a large component of the "emotional" in the project. I think there is with ours.

PEOPLE WITH DIFFERENT VANTAGE POINTS ON PATIENT CARE ALL HAVE DEMANDS, SO IT'S A REAL JUGGLING ACT TO COME UP WITH A BUILDING THAT IS PLEASANT FOR ALL.

What was the business case? It was pretty simple. It was the growth of the community and the need to create more capacity. We're in a very fast-growing county here, and we knew that in short order we were going to need more bed capacity and more operating room capacity, so that's what started it all. And then, as so often happens in these projects, we began to design strategic value into this building in addition to capacity. Some of it was the image change we wanted. We'd been in this community for 150 years, and people had a well-established opinion of what Southwest Washington Medical Center was. We wanted to change that, frankly.

Why? Our hospital had evolved through a number of iterations over the 150 years, and all of them reflected a modesty that I think started with the hospital's original little, log-cabin-like, wooden building. The architectural theme was always understated and quiet. I felt that it was time to change that. We had achieved significant accomplishments as a hospital. We had been named one of the top 100 hospitals six times, when there were only about 40 hospitals in the United States that had ever achieved that status. Yet, if you were to ask people around the Portland/Vancouver metropolitan area about us, they wouldn't be able to tell you where we were or even if we were here. So I wanted our new tower and our campus re-development to say, "Look at us. We're over here." We wanted to make a statement, architecturally, that was different from anything anybody had seen in Vancouver before.

What was your competition? We have a competitor about eight miles away. They have a new facility that's only been open for about a year and a half, built from scratch. One of the things we measured before we opened was: Are we going to lose medical staff? Are medical staff going to switch their loyalty to the other facility? Of course, hospitals have multiple constituencies. As well as medical staff we have patients, employees, and the public, all of great importance. This building was designed to try and maximize value to all of those constituencies.

What is the challenge of designing a new facility that meets the needs of all those different constituencies? The challenge is trying to make an environment that will keep physicians feeling good about their workplace, as well as employees and visitors. That is a daunting challenge because you have so many different professional people in a hospital. We have 175 different job categories, and that's not counting the physicians and the dozens of different specialties. We have so many people that come from different vantage points on patient care and they all have demands and expectations. So it's a real juggling act to come up with a building that is acceptable and pleasant for all those people. For example, the issue of floor coverings. The great debate is whether you should put carpet down, or a harder surface. The answers will vary 180 degrees depending on who you're talking with. If you're talking with a nurse who has to walk all day, he or she is

30%

INCREASE IN
ENERGY PERFORMANCE
BECAUSE OF ENHANCED
BUILDING SYSTEMS

E.W. & MARY
FIRSTENBURG
TOWE

PROJECT PROFILE

Southwest Washington Medical Center (SWMC) is the flagship provider for the Southwest Washington Health System, a regional network of six healthcare facilities across Washington State's Clark County.

Established in 1858, SWMC is one of the longest-running hospitals in the western United States. SWMC is a not-for-profit healthcare provider, governed and owned by the local community. Today, Southwest serves more than 200,000 patients per year in the Vancouver, Washington / Portland, Oregon region.

According to the 2007 U.S. Census Bureau Population Estimate, Clark County is the fifth largest and one of the fastest-growing counties in Washington state.

The new E.W. and Mary Firstenburg Tower is the first phase of a master plan that will help provide healthcare services to the area's rapidly growing and medically underserved population.

The 307,000-square-foot (28,500-square-meter), eight-story project includes a new Heart and Vascular Center, 15 new state-of-the-art surgery suites, six interventional suites, 144 new, private patient rooms, and a 3,370 square-foot (310-square-meter) outdoor garden for staff. The new facility makes SWMC one of the first hospitals in the country to offer a fully integrated service center that supports interventional radiology, cardiovascular, neurology, and open-heart services.

The project includes a new campus design that transforms a parking lot into healing gardens and landscaped community pathways. Three hundred varieties of trees and 3,000 plantings are dispersed among the campus' seven new gardens.

room 8105

12:54

S M T W T F S

going to say, "I want carpeting so my legs will hold up." If you're talking to a transportation aide, they're going to say, "Oh, we can't have carpet—I can't push carts and equipment over that." Even things you would think are as routine as what kind of floor surface there ought to be, they become difficult issues. They are resolved by including people in the design work. That was a major part of this project. We didn't do anything without consulting with nurses, physicians, the constituencies that were going to be in the space.

How did you do that consulting? We rented a warehouse in Vancouver during the planning of this. And we built plywood mockups of actual-sized patient rooms, and we moved equipment in. We brought our employees out and allowed them to experience the environment in 3D, to find out what we could improve upon, and of course we found all kinds of things. Hospitals are complicated spaces, and they're very expensive spaces, so you better make sure that every foot of your design makes sense.

And this mockup allowed you to be fairly confident, going into the later phases of the project, that it did make sense. It did. In fact, our rooms are consistently praised by our nurses. The classical managerial technique here is if you let

CHANGE DESIGN
TOOL IN ACTION

CHALLENGE ASSUMPTIONS

CREATE CHAMPIONS FOR THE VISION

BUILD RENAISSANCE TEAMS

EXPLORE THE EXPERIENCE

True performance-based design requires a variety of tools, used together, that are not part of the traditional design tool box. On Southwest Washington Medical Center, a sequence of tools — Challenge Assumptions, Create Champions for the Vision, Build Renaissance Teams, Explore the Experience — were used to enable change at many levels.

SEE PAGES 179, 187, 194, 196, FOR MORE INFORMATION ABOUT THESE TOOLS.

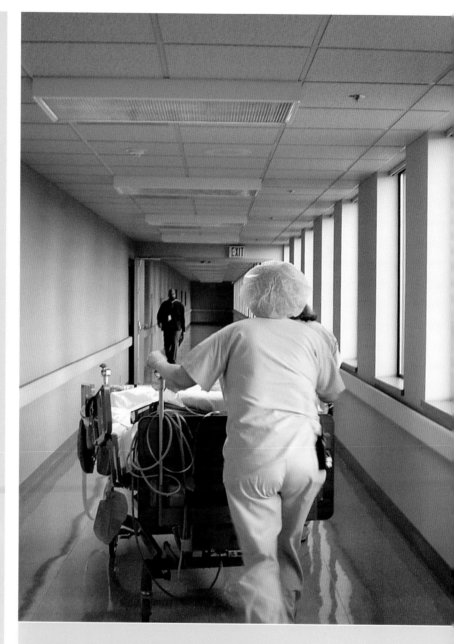

NO SACRED COWS

For Southwest Washington Medical Center, facing competition for the first time was a great motivator. It forced the entire team, from CEO to designers, to look at the hospital from new and different perspectives, which gave us insight into how the new building could better serve both external and internal customers. We asked ourselves, how do you organize an organization, convene an inclusive design team, and create processes to gain the insights that lead to performance-driven innovation?

CHALLENGE ASSUMPTIONS

It was clear to all of us that mere incremental improvements to the status quo wouldn't be enough in a rapidly changing healthcare market. We said: "No sacred cows," and organized ourselves to see SWMC and who they served and how they served through fresh eyes.

CREATE CHAMPIONS FOR THE VISION

Our process of engaging external customers and internal clients, and connecting our discoveries to design innovation, created champions for change, both within SWMC and the wider community. Because our process had demonstrated how individual experience could be improved by design, philanthropic support for this project reached an historic high.

BUILD RENAISSANCE TEAMS

We assessed the talent within the organization and the design team. We needed people with the skill to burrow deeper and wider into the current and the desired experience, and with the ability to communicate those insights in ways that inspired design innovation. We asked a psychologist with top experience in participatory research to lead our discovery team, and invited a respected experiential and industrial designer to co-design the discovery process.

EXPLORE THE EXPERIENCE

The complete discovery team included architectural, interior, and graphic designers; healthcare planners; a research psychologist; an anthro-pologist; and an experiential designer. Together they engaged both external customers (patients, families, and visitors) and internal clients (doctors, nurses, medical technologists, and staff), because for SWMC to succeed, both sets of needs had to be met. Deep insight takes time, so the team did several months of observational and participatory research. We created notebooks to rigorously capture experiential insights while separately recording design insights.

RICH DALLAM, PARTNER, NBBJ

people participate in the decision about it, they're going to be inclined to like it. So getting our nursing staff to accept the new room designs was a much easier task for management when, throughout our communications, we were able to genuinely remind our nurses that it was, frankly, their design. It was their input that helped create it; that they had literally pushed the bed around, pushed the IV poles around, moved the headboard placement around until we had reached a design everybody accepted.

Have you in fact been able to attract and retain staff the way you wanted to?
Well, take the doctors, for example. We did a rather sizable replacement of our operating room suites in this building, and we hoped our physicians would find working in our operating rooms superior to anything they could find in this community. And the early returns are great. Physicians are booking up all the available time we have. We had thought we would close down our old operating rooms once we were able to move into the new tower, but we are filling up capacity in the new tower, so we're having to keep our old operating rooms open as well. It's an expense we hadn't planned on, but it's nice to have problems like that.

What's been interesting for me is, every month I shadow one employee for a shift and follow them around. Sometimes I'll help do the work. Most of the time I'm not qualified, but I worked a shift with a young lady who was cleaning rooms. We cleaned a room in the old tower, then we did a room in the new tower. And it was interesting to see how the thoughtfulness of the design, even in terms of housekeeping, made cleaning the room easier. Even the texture of the surfaces on the cabinetry in the room had been evaluated by the housekeepers.

How often do you think hospitals actually consider their staff and their jobs in this way? I think everybody in healthcare is waking up to the fact that we have to keep our employees mentally healthy if we're going to expect them to deliver great care. For example, when nurses are surveyed nationally, hospitals are starting to come out as the more undesirable place for a nurse to work. With the nursing shortage, all of us need to be cognizant of the kind of work environment we create for our nurses. So we were very sensitive to that in the design of this building. One of the things we created for employees was a large open space that is enclosed, and reserved only for employees. It was designed to be a haven for employees to escape the stress of their work. At the time, it seemed like it might be an extravagance; in hindsight, I'm very glad we did it. A lot of the design features we put into our operating area, windows to provide external circulation and outside light, also turned out to be wonderful. For staff, who work in a stressful operating room environment, to be able to step out between cases and immediately be bathed with outside light and a view—I've received numerous compliments from employees who are very grateful that we considered the stress of the job in the way the space was designed. It's nice that they noticed. When I walk down the staircase in the lobby and look at our outdoor, running-water stream with waterfalls and little sitting areas, I love it when I see employees sitting out there taking their breaks. I want to stock the stream with trout and go out there at lunch and cast a little fly! I don't think they're going to let me do that, but the sound of the water, the way the rocks tie into the stone inside the lobby, I think our employees, and the public, get the architectural plan.

What are you hearing from the public? What are your clues that they are in fact responding to the hospital in a different way now? Whenever I talk to people in the community, as soon as they find out that I work for Southwest, the next sentence always contains some reference to our building, to the look, to the community pride now that we're here.

60,000
SQUARE FEET OF GLASS FLOODS THE HOSPITAL WITH NATURAL LIGHT FOR QUICKER HEALING AND INCREASED PRODUCTIVITY.

The community played a significant role in making this project possible. Well, it was expensive to build. We have a project here that, if you include the equipment, was over $150 million to construct. We started a fund-raising campaign in the community, and we set a goal of raising $50 million. Now, in this community, the most that had ever been raised before was $3 million. So people thought we were crazy, that it couldn't be done. But when this building started coming out of the ground and people could see what was going to happen, it was amazing. Leaders in the community, people who had the resources to write two-comma checks, the idea of having their name or their family tradition associated with this building became very appealing. We raised $53 million, which for our community was unprecedented.

What a terrific endorsement of what you were doing. I agree. That's the way I felt about it, too. It was the ultimate endorsement of what we were trying to achieve: To wake up the community and give them a sense of pride in this healthcare facility.

As Chief Operating Officer for Southwest Washington Medical Center (SWMC), Renate Atkins is responsible for overseeing all of SWMC's operations, including all clinical, technical, and support services, site and facility planning, and service improvement initiatives. Prior to joining SWMC in 2003, Atkins was the Vice President of Operations at Verde Valley Medical Center in northern Arizona, and held various director-level positions for the Northern Arizona Healthcare System and Flagstaff Medical Center, Arizona. Atkins is a registered nurse and holds a Master of Health Services Administration from St. Joseph's College, Maine, and a Bachelor of Science in Nursing from Northern Arizona University.

RENATE M. ATKINS
CHIEF OPERATING OFFICER, SOUTHWEST WASHINGTON MEDICAL CENTER

The plan to build the new tower began with you and the design team going through an evaluation process. What was your goal for that? We wanted to see where the flaws and the gaps were in service, in patient perception, in staff flow, before we even began to design this building. Everything we have tried to do is based on maximizing a sense of respect and comfort for patient, for family, and for staff. When you look at what drives patient and family comfort in a hospitalized environment, one of the things that has been really important to me is, first of all, very few people come to the hospital to have a holiday. Most people come to the hospital because they need some kind of an elective procedure or because they're really sick. So the kind of environment that we want to create needs to take things from your home environment that bring you comfort, and try to infuse as much of that as possible into the patient care experience: Easy access to your loved ones for communication; light in your space; sounds that are abated; the capability for color, for artwork that's personalized for you; for privacy, for spaciousness, enough room around you that you don't feel like you're going to trip. You have to ask the question, "What do you need to provide a safe environment for patients, physicians, and staff?" as well as, "How do you create an environment that is also comfortable and healing?"

How did you and the design team go about designing an environment that is comfortable? The comfort side is trying to see the hospital from a patient's and family's viewpoint. What does it feel like to be rolled around in a gurney down the hall? How do the lights feel when you're being rolled around? How does it feel when your stretcher is going over the transition between a carpet and a hard floor surface in the room? All these things were considered in the design. We know that there are several things that really make a huge difference for patients and families. External lighting is very important. Even when you're sick you need to be cognizant of the transition between day and night, light and dark. We didn't want a long corridor on the patient care unit sides; we didn't want it to feel like a big open bay hospital of the 1950s. We wanted to cantilever the rooms a little bit so that each space felt more intimate, more secure, more homey.

We have all had the experience where we're visiting a loved one in the hospital and the doctor or nurse comes into the room and wants to have a conversation with that patient, and you may not be immediate family, and you need to leave the room. Where do you go? Well, in this particular environment, through some good thinking from everybody, we designed a little perch outside of the room where family members can have a seat and be comfortable while a conversation is going on inside the room. They don't feel displaced, they don't feel pushed to a waiting room that may be 25 or 35 feet down the hall. Or if you need some air or want to go for a walk, what better thing to do than to go out and have a seat by the "river-of-caring," a beautiful landscaped fountain on the hospital grounds. We wanted to provide places, both inside and out, where families would feel comfortable.

How does the design of the new entrance lobby play into this? We wanted to send the message: Thank you for choosing us, thank you for being here, we're going to take good care of you. I believe a hospital environment should portray a sense of welcome, confidence, and comfort. The last thing you want to do is to make a lobby or a main entry space so technically cold that it doesn't feel welcoming. So when you first walk into our building, there is this beautiful, open space with warm colors and easy wayfinding. There's also a wonderful café and a flower shop.

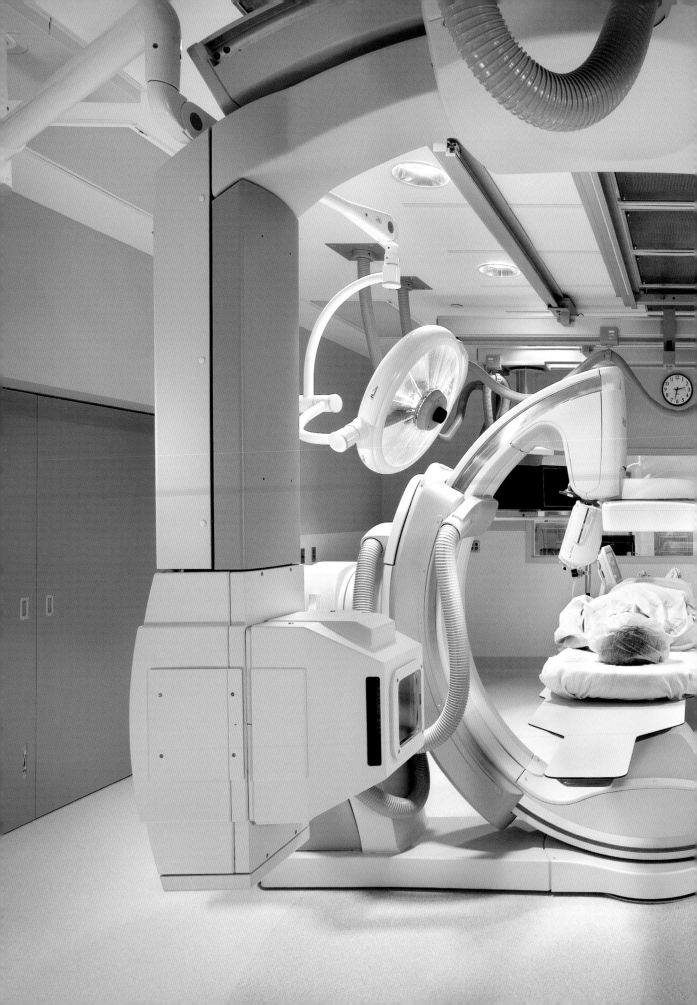

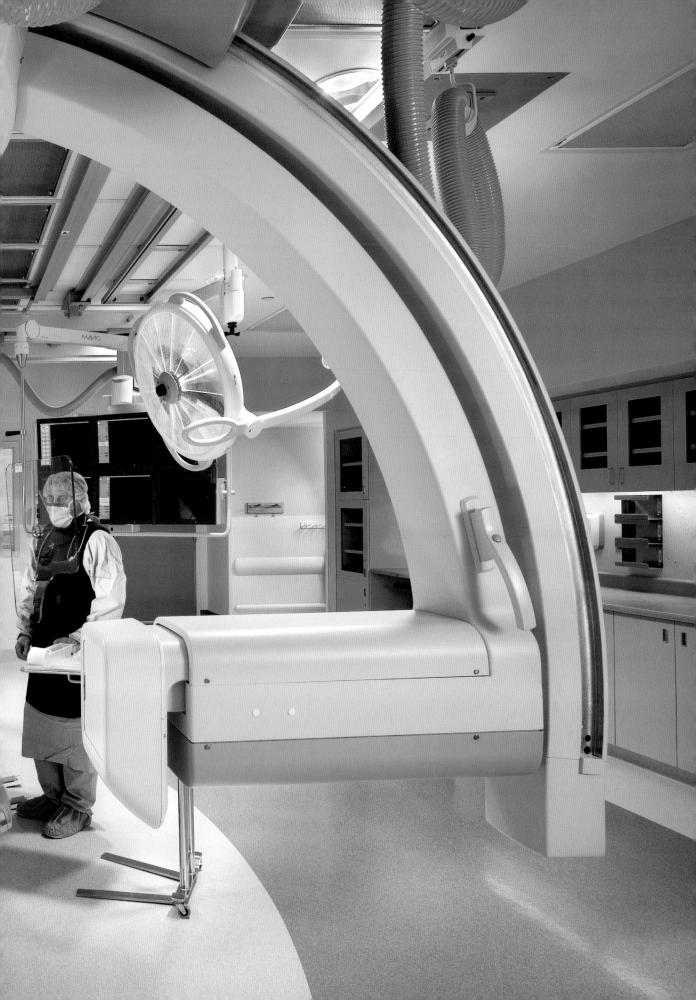

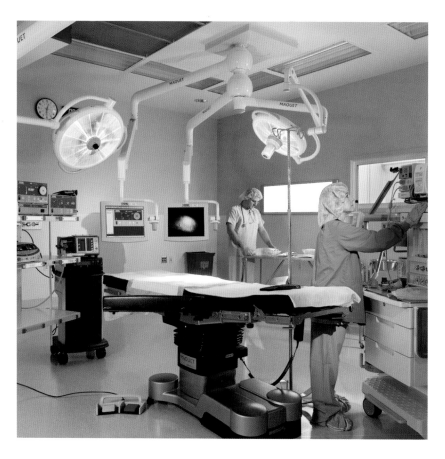

What does all of that mean? It means comfort. It means life being brought in. It means my senses are filled, and I feel welcome. When we did open houses and tours, people would walk into the building and they would kind of stop breathing for a minute. Not because they needed to go to the emergency department but because there was such a sense of warm grandeur about the space.

You mentioned the need for safety—why is safety such a critical consideration not only for hospital functioning but also for hospital design? Well, we know that patients get hurt where there is any kind of a gap, where a patient goes from one place in a facility to another place in the facility. It's not that we intend to hurt patients during that period of time, but if hurt is going to occur it's going to occur during those hand-offs or gaps in care. Therefore, what you want to try to develop is a standardized environmental approach to where you situate things.

Think about it this way: You function based on the signals in the environment around you. What would you do if a stoplight was red one time, if it was yellow another time, and if it was green yet another time? What would you do if purple, or orange, or any other color were added in there? So what we wanted to do is decrease the variability in how we do our work with our patients.

When we considered the patient rooms, we made sure that everything that we did in the patient room was always on the right side of the nurse or the left side of the nurse. What is on the right side in Room A, is on the right side in Room B, and the right side in Room C, and the right side in Room D. It isn't on the right side in Room A, and the left side in Room B, and the right side in Room C. This consistency helps protect patient safety. When we designed the patient care bathroom, we didn't design it at a high level. We involved both physical therapists and nursing staff, who practiced how many pivots a patient would have to make to move from the bed to the chair, from the chair to rise, from that rise in the chair to the bathroom where they could have access to the toilet and to the wash basin. We designed that access with the least number of pivots and turns,

EVERYTHING IS BASED ON MAXIMIZING A SENSE OF RESPECT AND COMFORT FOR PATIENTS, FAMILY AND STAFF.

because obviously, the more pivots and turns that you have, the higher the risk for falls, the higher the risk for injury.

For every piece of the design we thought through those kinds of issues. Simple things like doors that are a foot-and-a-half, almost two-feet wider than a normal patient room door. If you're a patient being wheeled into your room post-operatively, you're going to have less chance of being bumped against a wall as you're swung into your room. Those little things make a difference for the clinical staff, too, because they don't have such a tight curve as they're trying to push the bed into the right location. We have prevented back injury to staff and we have prevented unnecessary pain for the patient.

What culture changes did these design changes mean for staff? You develop the way you do your work based on the environment you work in. We got a lot of help from the design team to help us understand what the impacts of the design would be, because what you don't want to do when you design and build a new building is take flawed work processes and import them. You really need to look at your objectives and how you're going to do that work. What are the complexities that you face on a day-to-day basis?

Let me give you an example. In the old Intensive Care Unit, to get a new bag of solution for an IV, a nurse had to bend down, open up the computerized door of the medication locker, take a bag of fluid out of the refrigerator—these could be one-liter or two-liter bags, they're fairly heavy—then go and hang it on the patient. How much did the nurse have to bend to pick up that bag? Is that the right ergonomic position for doing that work? How many steps did that process take? What you want to do is carve the wasted processes out of the workflow.

So there was a tremendous amount of attention on workflow, a lot of observation of work; a lot of testing; a lot of analyzing; re-testing. And we worked with the design team all the way through the process. It was great having experts in clinical practice be collaborators in the design process, working together with the architects to design the future of their organization. When you're designing a hospital for the community you live in and work in, you're not just designing for someone you don't know. The hospital will be used by or will touch your family—the people that you care about deeply.

NET WORKS

At the California Institute for Telecommunications and Information Technology at UC San Diego, Larry Smarr links scientists and artists in a new kind of team building.

LARRY SMARR

DIRECTOR, CALIFORNIA INSTITUTE FOR TELECOMMUNICATIONS
AND INFORMATION TECHNOLOGY (CALIT2)

In addition to being founding director of Calit2, Larry Smarr is also the Harry E. Gruber professor in the Jacobs School's Department of Computer Science and Engineering at UCSD, the Principal Investigator on the National Science Foundation (NSF) OptIPuter LambdaGrid project, and Co-PI on the NSF LOOKING ocean observatory prototype. As founding director of the National Center for Super-computing Applications (1985) and the National Computational Science Alliance (1997), Smarr has driven major contributions to the development of the national information infrastructure: the Internet, the Web, the emerging Grid, collaboratories, and scientific visualization. He was a member of the President's Information Technology Advisory Committee and serves on the Advisory Committee to the Director of the National Institutes of Health and the NASA Advisory Council.

The State of California launched an initiative in 2000 to ensure that it stayed at the forefront of technological innovation. This was one of the sparks that led to the creation of Calit2. Why was the university drawn to this initiative? The University of California is, in a sense, more like 10 universities than one university. If all 10 campuses worked together, there'd really be no other university in the world that could compete. But, in fact, the 10 are isolated from each other, intellectually as well as physically. Many of them—Berkeley, UCLA, San Diego—are world class; however, they became world class by hiring individual faculty, and basing promotion around individuals. If you want your papers counted, they'd better be single-author.

On the other hand, the problems that California faces are systemic problems—transportation, the environment, earthquakes, and so forth. These aren't like single-author papers. The University of California realized that if it could come up with a persistent horizontal collaborative framework that could pull together researchers from different disciplines and attack larger-scale problems, ones that would involve industry, or would be actualized out in the community, then they would get much more productivity out of their investment in buildings and faculty.

They envisioned four institutes that would be collaborative by nature. They wouldn't just build a building and bring in a bunch of superstars and let them do their own thing. Instead, it was a social engineering experiment. Each institute was focused on an area that was very fast-changing: QB3 is focused on quantitative biology; CNSI on nanosystems, and ours, Calit2, is focused on the future of the Internet. To a large extent, California's economy depends on that.

THE CHALLENGE WAS, HOW DO WE PUT INTO ARCHITECTURE A PERSISTENT COLLABORATIVE FRAMEWORK?

We received $100 million to build two buildings and 70 percent of that was going to the building here at the University of California, San Diego [UCSD]. The challenge was to put a persistent collaborative framework into architecture.

The formal mission of the institute is to extend the reach of the Internet throughout the physical world. That's a big mission. What did you figure it would take to accomplish this? We knew we needed more than people working on just bits and bytes. We needed the end user communities that were going to be transformed by the future of the Internet—people in electrical engineering, the environment, transportation, biomedical research, digital cinema, and networked computer games.

We decided that we would focus on integrating the component parts that the individual faculties and their students represent into working, large-scale systems of the future.

I invented what I called "living laboratories of the future." Now, you might think, "How can you invent the future, because if you've invented it, isn't it already part of the present?" For instance, your PC now is a gigahertz PC. I had my first gigahertz computer in 1988 and it cost $15 million. It took from 1988 until about 2003 for the cost of multi-gigahertz computers to come down to mass market affordability. We can build living laboratories of the future on technologies that are at the top of their cost curve and are coming down.

So when you're talking about the future you're talking about what the average person would perceive as futuristic. Exactly, because that's how people see it. The Internet started in '72. The protocols were written in 1990, 15 years ago. And yet you ask anybody, "When did the Web start?" and they say, "Oh, it's been great the last five years," because that's people's perception. When a technology has exponential growth, it crosses the threshold of public perception and people finally notice it.

So, the question was, how could we build a building that would do three things: provide an internal and external architecture that would signify the future; encourage collaboration between people who are, in the rest of their professional lives, in an architectural environment that fosters individual work; and create laboratories and facilities that would be unique not only on our campus but on many campuses.

So when NBBJ said, "What exactly do you want in this building?" I said, "I want it to be an enchanted castle."

An enchanted castle? Think about all the Walt Disney movies you've seen with enchanted castles. What makes them odd is that inanimate objects talk to you. They're not alive, but you're in a world that is active, in which data is everywhere.

In our case, we want to do teamwork, but a lot of the team members aren't here in California. Instead of having a whiteboard on one wall in a room, you have 50-inch plasma panels. It's not a TV, it's a window, to your office, or the office of a colleague in Singapore, Toronto, or Amsterdam. It doesn't matter where, because with worldwide fiber optics and high-definition video you have tele-presence. Instead of looking out your window and seeing what is physically several feet on the other side of the window, you can see anywhere in the world.

PROJECT PROFILE

The California Institute for Telecommunications and Information Technology (Calit2) is one of four research institutes launched in 2000 through the California Institutes for Science and Innovation initiative.

Calit2 focuses its work in the context of telecommunications and information technology as they relate to the evolving Internet. The institute is conducting research in nanotechnology, life sciences, information technology, and telecommunications (wireless and optical).

Calit2 commissioned two buildings at UC San Diego and UC Irvine to realize its technological and social goals. Funding for the Calit2 buildings came from California taxpayers as part of the state's $100 million startup investment in the institute and was conditioned on Calit2 raising at least twice as much from other sources.

Since December 2000, Calit2 faculty members have received more than $226 million in federal research awards. industry and research donations total approximately $78 million to date.

Calit2 constitutes one of the largest multidisciplinary research centers in the nation. At peak capacity, the new research building, Atkinson Hall, at UCSD, will house 900 researchers and staff, most of them working on projects led by faculty from more than 20 campus departments.

The research projects under Calit2's aegis bring together experts who typically would not be housed under the same roof, much less in adjacent labs.

How did you get from the castle metaphor to the building you now have?
Through many discussions with NBBJ and the faculty that would be in it. Two
dozen departments have faculty in the building. We had artists, chemists, engineers, medical doctors sitting around talking about the layout and shape of the
building. One of the amazing things is that NBBJ tore up and redid the entire
volumetric layout of the building at least three times, because they kept seeing
new pieces. We would say we had to have a state-of-the-art digital theater, we had
to have a set of nanotechnology clean rooms, we had to have circuit labs and
radio labs and photonics labs, and we had to have performance art spaces. And
they would say, "Okay. This is really great! We've never put all these functions
into any one building. In fact, nobody has ever done that."

And you're making the future. Yes. So what is it about the future that would tell
an architect something? Namely, that they can't possibly know what we're going to
be working on five or 10 years from now, and the building's going to be around
for probably 50 or 100 years, so flexibility was the most important thing. We had
to have it so that when you looked at a laboratory you couldn't tell what it was
for, because if you could it was too specific, and might be obsolete.

**And you also have a situation where the actual population of the building is
changing all the time, as well?** Yes. The UCSD building will house about 900
people. At least three-quarters of them are students, so they're constantly turning
over. The space is allocated based on projects and there are about 50 projects at
any one time. When your projects are done, you're gone.

And then...? Maybe you've got a new project.

**But it'll be an entirely different use of the space, either by you or by another
group.** That's right.

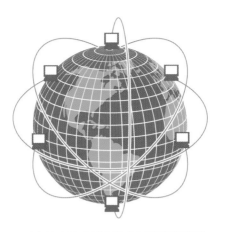

LOCAL AND GLOBAL CONNECTIVITY:
Networking and collaboration are the backbone of Calit2's mission. The building's infrastructure contains two million square feet of ethernet cable, which allows consistent and rapid connections with UCSD campus networks and collaborators worldwide.

You've been referring to performance spaces as though there was nothing unusual about having them in a science building, but in fact, putting artists and scientists next to each other in the same space is not the way things are typically done. Why was that important to your mission? I've always worked with digital artists, even though I'm a computer scientist and physicist myself. Society has artists for a lot of reasons, but one reason is that they're like the canary in the coal mine. They detect the future first. And anything that will help us understand earlier where the future is coming from is to our advantage. Another reason is that the technology we're working with is socially disruptive. You could argue that the fall of the Soviet Union would, to a large extent, have been impossible without the Internet and fax machines. In the United States, we're concerned about the permissible limits of the use of our ubiquitous sensor technology. How does society form laws and regulations and customs in an entirely new space in which privacy is an obsolete notion? Artists deal with all of this stuff.

So you're working not just with the technology but with the implications of the possible uses of the technology. Very much. That is, in some ways, the most important part of the future. Look at what Napster did to disrupt the record industry.

However, I'm the first high scientist on this campus who has ever paid any attention—much less given any resources—to the digital artists. The University of California's Center for Research Computing in the Arts is one of the two most long-lived digital arts groups of any university in the United States. It's been going for 30 years. These guys were used to living underground, because nobody cared about them, and I come in and put $10 to $15 million worth of the best facilities in the country in their hands. This building has tremendous visual art capabilities. We have digital spatialized audio labs, motion capture labs that the dance instructors use, a black box theater, a digital theater lab, and a giant virtual reality room. Sony is putting the first of its high-resolution digital cinema projectors in the United States in our building. Who's going to make the content? Not the engineers. It would be really boring in that theater if it was solely a bunch of engineers.

Of course there's this incredible clash between the artists' culture and the science and engineering culture. But, amazingly, when you talk to our artists and ask, "What are you into?" They say, "Well, these guys here on the same floor showed us what they could do with microscopes, so we're thinking a lot about nanoart." This is the kind of crazy mixing that we wanted to happen and that the architecture lets happen.

You're describing how the artists are being inspired by things they've seen in the scientific labs. Are you seeing a flow in the other direction, back to the scientists? Very much so. What the scientists need from the artists is new visual metaphors. Let's say the scientists are trying to represent network traffic. Do you represent it physically where the fiber cables are, or do you represent it abstractly in some sort of communications space? There is no physical object that is network traffic, so there's no preconceived visual notion of what it would look like. The artists become part of these teams. They do some really interesting visual thing with the data. They're innovating in the abstract space of representation. Over the years, I have found this to be invaluable to the scientist.

This has been done before but not in a way that has been planned for, which is what you've done here with the Institute. Yes. I took everything I've learned over the years and tried to take it from being an odd thing that had happened to something that the architecture would make more common.

The *New York Times* calls what you've created a "collaboratory." As far as I know, that term was coined about 10 to 15 years ago by Bill Wulf, who's currently the president of the National Academy of Engineering in the U.S. He was in charge of the computer science division of the National Science Foundation when he came up with the term.

There have been very few examples of collaboratories. What you're trying to build is an environment in which people can easily work together regardless of where they are in physical space. That means not just that you can see each other's PowerPoints, but that you can visualize any digital material on the fly.

Say you're working on environmental sensor nets and you've got photos coming in from a wetland. The fundamental things that you're sensing are humidity and wind velocity and salinity. How do you turn those back into a visual representation that can be shared over the network with biologists, chemists, and the people who built the network? You may have to bring in satellite imagery, and overlay that with actual sensor feeds and so on. The whole Calit2 building is set up to enable that.

You're talking about creating a network that is extending well beyond the walls of the building itself. Very much so. That's why many of the living laboratories of the future are built in the community. For instance, we've been funded by the National Science Foundation to work with the first-responder community— the police and fire and emergency—to build an instrumented gas-lamp district. The Gas-Lamp Quarter is a famous tourist attraction in San Diego and it tends to hold large events in which there are 50,000 people milling around. Occasionally there are fights and disruptions that could hurt a lot of people if the first-responders don't know about them early, so we're working with the city to evaluate which of the various technologies you could put there both to aid the first-responders and support citizens' right to privacy.

We'll be in the Gas-Lamp Quarter shimmying up light poles, putting up technology that was developed in our building. Parts of our building are set up as advanced versions of this technology. They test the software integration and ensure that the technology is going to work if it gets rained on. The fiddling around and vetting part goes on in the building, but the deployment part of our living labs tends to be out in the community.

Was WiFi connectivity an important factor for the building because of this kind of work with the outside world? The entire building has high-bandwidth wireless and it isn't just for PCs or PDAs. We want to be able to put a temperature, humidity, or light sensor anywhere, and these come with miniature WiFi antennae. WiFi is still pretty low bandwidth compared to current gigabit Ethernet. We also have 1.8 million feet of gigabit Ethernet cable in the building, enough for 9,000 gigabit Ethernet drops—10 gigabit drops per person.

How did the design of the building morph in order to accommodate these needs? We had to look at the wireless transparency of the building. We evaluated materials for the ducts, the walls, and the façade depending on their transparency in the gigahertz radio band. Normally, you don't think about the electromagnetic environment of a building, or about how metal interferes with it being a conductor. There's something called a Faraday cage, which is made of wire mesh. Electromagnetic waves don't propagate inside of that cage. What we wanted was an "anti-Faraday cage." We wanted to have signals propagating throughout the building. The architects spent a lot of time on the way the building's interior steel frame was laid out, and we chose Trespa, a composite material, for the exterior to minimize the blocking of electromagnetic waves.

CHANGE DESIGN
TOOL IN ACTION

BUILD RENAISSANCE TEAMS

A diversity of intelligence yields a greater opportunity for high-performance outcomes. That maxim drove the development of the NBBJ Change Tool "Build Renaissance Teams." On the Calit2 project, the tool promoted us to use multiple lenses to see through complex problems.

SEE PAGE 194 FOR MORE INFORMATION ABOUT THIS TOOL.

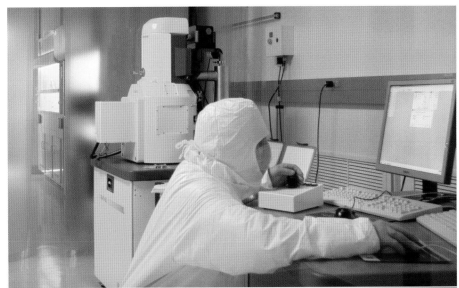

LABORATORY DRAMA

In designing research buildings, the number one guideline is: don't preclude the opportunity to conduct the research, and number two is: find ways of building in a robust system for exploring the opportunities and enhancing the communication of people who are there. That's why on this project—really on any project—we work as a team from the beginning with people who create the future. We're constantly developing and testing and doing a lot of scenario planning—what would happen if they wanted to do this, and what would happen if they wanted to do that. It's a very iterative process where you test and redraw and test and manipulate and tweak and go back and forth, and eventually, together, you get to the point where the design's ready to be built.

There was a long list of consultants on this project, including people who you wouldn't normally pull into an architectural team for a research building, such as acousticians, and data and media experts who do sound reinforcement and design projection and sound systems. We also brought in theater consultants. The team came up with three major media spaces. There's the 150-seat theater, which will work in at least six configurations, from a formal musical theater to a digital cinema. The multi-use room has modular seating risers that can be arranged any way you want. And the black box is... I guess the best way to conceive of it is like the holo-deck in *Star Trek*—it's a virtual reality chamber. All those spaces are the work of our "Renaissance Team."

BRAD LEATHLEY, PRINCIPAL, NBBJ

I WANTED PEOPLE TO SEE THE INFRASTRUCTURE, THE BARE BONES AND CIRCULATORY SYSTEM OF THE BUILDING ITSELF, SO THAT THEY WOULD THINK ABOUT INFRASTRUCTURE ON A DAILY BASIS.

The other thing about the interior is that there are no drop ceilings. When you look up you see the steam pipes, water pipes, and Ethernet trays. There were a couple of reasons we did that. One was the ease of access, but another was so that when people look around the building they see infrastructure. Imagine if your skin was transparent and you could see the infrastructure of your circulatory, nervous, and digestive systems. Right now we look like black boxes, so people don't think about the intricate systems inside us. Since we're about the future of information infrastructure, I wanted people to see the infrastructure, the bare bones and circulatory system of the building itself, so that they would think about infrastructure on a daily basis.

I've heard the building referred to as rough around the edges by design. Is that what you're getting at? Yes. On the one hand, when people look at the building from the outside, they think it's very futuristic. But when they're inside, they see all of this infrastructure and they sometimes say, "Why didn't they finish that off so it looks nice?" and I say, "Because we are information infrastructure engineers. Infrastructure is us. We think infrastructure's interesting, so we don't want to hide it."

You want to be able to see how everything works. And how intricate it is. Everything about human society these days, at least in the developed world, is devoted to hiding all the little things that make the world work. I sometimes think if it wasn't for the people who actually service the infrastructure, we'd all be doomed. We'd never know how to fix anything. Our whole world is held together by infrastructure, and we want our students to think infrastructure when they go out in the world.

You talked earlier about the Institute as a social engineering experiment. If it's an experiment, what's your hypothesis? My sense is that the natural state of the world is for people to work in teams of different specialties. But for the past hundred years, the university has gone down this path of extreme reductionism in which they break everything down into the tiniest little components, and then you're a specialist in that. I like to say that we put the "uni" back in "university."

When Bob Dynes, the president of the University of California, came to the dedication of Calit2, he said that these institutes are the future of universities, and that Calit2 is at the point of the spear, because it is able to naturally form and unform, in an effervescent fashion over time, self-selecting teams to attack major problems. If universities learn how to do that, they're going to be incredibly valuable to society. And our students will come out assuming that's the way the world works. So they are our chief social engineering export. We want them to spread the disease.

We developed a layer-cake diagram for the building. We invented it because people said, "You're all over the map. How do you add up to anything coherent?" I said, "At the base level we're talking about new materials and new devices, the

I STOP PEOPLE IN THE HALL AND SAY, "HOW'S IT GOING?" AND THEY SAY, "IT'S JUST SO FREE. YOU CAN THINK AND INVENT."

very tiny things that form the insides of everything—cellphones, sensors, the electrical systems in cars, the insides of televisions and radios. Then the next level up is the wireless and the optical networking that ties those things together with the Internet. The next layer above that are the different embedded software systems in your processors, cellphone, operating system on your PC, and so forth that make the Internet run. The top layer is the social transformations driven by the underlying technologies. What are the social, regulatory, and ethical evolutions that occur?

And just to clarify the layers, you're talking about conceptual, organizational, and even physical layers. As I talked to NBBJ about this they said, "Well, won't the networking guys just stay in their own layer? How will you get them to go vertically to talk to the environment people?" The diagram is stratified horizontally and the layers are floors. The living labs form these vertical conductive currents. In other words, if you're going to build an intelligent transportation test bed out in the freeways, you're going to need software people, networking people, and device people. These projects will create vertical currents that will automatically and naturally mix. They'll go in and select out of the layers the people they need, and they'll start having team meetings, and those team meetings will be vertical.

NBBJ translated that idea into the very architecture of the building, so if you look at it from the outside you'll see vertical rectangular forms that slide across floors in different ways. When I asked NBBJ what they were, they said, "Those are your vertical convective currents that are connecting the layers."

It sounds like the project to design the building was a collaboratory. Absolutely. That was critical to the successful outcome. The design of the building itself was the most important formative aspect of creating Calit2 as it exists today, because it forced people at an early stage to come together from all these different disciplines, respect and listen to each other's opinion, and collectively make decisions. It formed our cultural DNA.

And set the conditions for what you were going to be doing once the physical structure existed. It built a lot of the early culture. You look at this building and then you go around and look at the other university buildings and you say, "Wow, how come these other buildings look so shabby by comparison?" It's because they have no freedom to innovate. In this building, I stop people in the hall and ask, "How's it going?" and they say, "Oh, it's so great to be here working at Calit2." When I ask, "Why?" they answer, "It's just so free, you can think and invent and make things happen. It's not clamped-down and bureaucratic the way the rest of the university is."

CHANGE DESIGN ESSAYS

To link this book to the wider conversation happening about performance-based design, Change Design invited a group of writers, consultants, academics, and designers who have been thinking about the subject to a round table conducted by e-mail. Participants included author Daniel Pink; architect and former U.S. ambassador Richard Swett; workplace consultant Alexi Marmot; business school professor Jeanne Liedtka; and business school dean Roger Martin. Their thinking, along with that of medical doctor Astrid Pujari and Bruce Mau Design's Creative Director, Bruce Mau, is captured here in a series of Change Design Essays.

DANIEL PINK

The author of *The Adventures of Johnny Bunko: The Last Career Guide You'll Ever Need* and *A Whole New Mind*, a book about the rise of right-brain thinking in modern economies, Daniel Pink also writes on work, design, and economic transformation for many publications, including *The New York Times*, *Harvard Business Review*, *Fast Company*, and *Wired*, where he is a contributing editor.

What is design? I'll fall back on the easy (and perhaps simplistic) definition: design is utility combined with significance. Utility without significance is a forgettable functionality. Significance without utility is mere ornamentation.

Why does that definition matter with regard to the design of humane, productivity-enhancing workspaces? My first instinct is to say that workspaces have sacrificed one aspect of our definition on the altar of the other. What is a cubicle farm, after all, except a triumph of utility over significance? But I don't think that's fair. In my travels and reporting, I've seen many organizations that seem sincere in trying to create better work environments. There's a growing mainstream recognition that significance can enhance utility—and a realization that the most talented workers want a workspace that is more appealing and uplifting than acres of dreary cubicles sprouting from a landscape of gray carpet. I truly believe that many organizations desire to create better workplaces. The reason they fail is that they don't know how.

The reason they don't know how is because they've accepted a cheapened form of significance handed to them by the descendants of American architect Frank Lloyd Wright, who screwed his furniture to the floor of his buildings so that people didn't mess up his handiwork. Today's corporate men and women are not as aggressively disdainful of human beings as the great master was, but they're often just as woefully clueless. People matter. That's a trite sentiment, I know, but it's often neglected in the pursuit of the hip, the nifty, and the photogenic.

What, then, are the skills that matter most? Two come to mind. One skill is "boundary crossing." Many people in business are very uncomfortable crossing into different domains. Their expertise is so great in one area that they feel like amateurs in other domains—and therefore avoid them. But that approach no longer works. It's a multi-world. The rewards go to the multidisciplinary, the multilingual, the multifaceted. And if people matter (not just in the touchy-feely sense, but to the bottom line), the second key skill is empathy—seeing with someone else's eyes and feeling with someone else's heart. This is a consummate design skill, of course. But empathy is moving to the core of business—because working in outwardly beautiful buildings where people can't connect and where they can't reach their potential is not much better than being stuck in row 14, cube nine of a Dilbertian workspace. But infusing all aspects of business with greater empathy—for employees, for customers, for each other—that can change the world. Empathy is both effective and transcendent—the ultimate combination of utility and significance.

BRUCE MAU

As founder of Bruce Mau Design Inc., a studio with international recognition for innovation across a wide range of projects, Bruce Mau collaborates with some of the world's leading architects and institutions, artists and entrepreneurs, academics and businesses. His book *Massive Change*, produced in collaboration with The Institute Without Boundaries, explores the changing force of design in the contemporary world.

For me, one of the big questions is: What is the future of the workplace? Is the workplace an office or a studio? Is the workplace a place where you can spill things? If you can't spill things, you've got a problem.

We can now look with a certain amount of clarity at the 20th century and see what happened to modernity, and in some ways what happened was the Henry Ford concept of breaking things into expertise, into pieces that you could optimize.

In architecture that meant that the building became the project. But in fact, if you go back into the history of architecture, the building isn't the project. How to live—and work—is the project. So, another big question arises: How do you get from 20th century architectural practice back to more holistic thinking?

There is an arrogance in the classical understanding of design, and you can see its legacy in different fields. For instance, with every hospital you go into, the designers, it seems, were absolutely convinced it would be the last hospital ever designed; this was it, they had finally figured it out! That's because in the past century architecture has, for the most part, been conceived of as "hardware," the physical, material, fixed part of an operating system. In fact, what we now know is that architecture isn't hardware; it's software. It's a software platform that supports applications; what you're really designing when you're designing a building is not a stable resolution but a dynamic equilibrium. To go back to my example, in hospitals you cannot know the innovation that will happen in medical science in the years to come, and you must design the platform with that in mind. You have to say, "Well, our real job is change, and supporting it in the long term." So the new hospital is version 1.0, and there will be 2.0, and 3.0. You're making something that has to hold together as a platform, but the real ambition is to sustain ongoing evolution.

It takes a lot more courage to do that than to do what most people think of when they think of architecture. It takes a totally different methodology and sensibility. One of the things to keep in mind is that everything communicates. A building tells a story without words. You're either communicating intentionally or it's like a garden hose without a sprinkler: everything will get wet eventually but it's going to be ugly. When you realize that everything is speaking, you realize an environment is talking all the time. And a lot of that talking—not only in environments but in companies generally—is mumbling and grumbling and whispered complaints. It's just under the audible tone, but it's the wrong message.

I believe that the opportunity is to make that message a song, to make it sing about value and potential and possibilities. Because holistic design methodology begins with this thought: "Anything is possible."

JEANNE LIEDTKA

Professor of Business Administration at the University of Virginia's Darden Graduate School of Business Administration and former Executive Director of the Batten Institute at Darden, Jeanne Liedtka is the author of many papers on design and business, including "In Defense of Strategy as Design" in the *California Management Review.*

We have much to learn from buildings that are spectacular failures—not minor, thoughtless buildings, boxes with no fore-thought given to them. I mean buildings that were lavishly designed but that seem to lack any facilitative connection to their ostensible purpose. These are the beautiful buildings that we admire as we pass through, buildings that seem to co-exist alongside of us but that we never really inhabit.

I know such a building. It is gorgeous, recently built on a venerable American university campus, and meant to evoke in a very literal way Thomas Jefferson's idea of the "Academical Village"—lawn, covered porticos and all. However, it is full of hallways that dead-end and separate buildings for faculty and students. Those who work there say the sense of disconnection and loss of interaction that accompanied the move into the new quarters was palpable. The old building, on the other hand, was a hideous '70s-era bunker—but it had corridors that circled, it squashed its inhabitants together, and, for those inhab-itants, operated and felt like Jefferson's learning community in a way that they feel the new building, built so deliberately to look like Jefferson's, never will. It represents building as symbol, decoupled from any deep understanding of specific purpose. It is, it seems, a type of building that we all love to look at, and only discover the deficiencies of when it's time to move in.

Perhaps very little of the fault lies with the designer. If the client has no clear sense of the kind of behaviors they want their space to evoke, then it is no surprise that built environments reflect that lack of specificity. This would certainly be true of many business organizations. Consider the enormous popularity and endurance of the Dilbert-like cubicle. Was there ever a design so superficially functional and yet utterly soulless? A padded cell in exchange for the illusion of privacy and flexibility.

This desire for flexibility often takes the easy way out, settling for bland spaces that give little thought to any one pur-pose in their rush to accommodate many purposes. The specificity that makes great design so engaging is sacrificed. Designs endure when they get the basics—the understanding of a particular set of human needs and wants—right. That takes a level of disciplined forethought on the part of both the client and the designer that is, I suppose, rather rare, both in the world of architecture and in the world of business.

ALEXI MARMOT

AMA Alexi Marmot Associates offers high-level advice to organizations with complex space and people issues. Founder Alexi Marmot is a London-based architect, workplace consultant, and author of the book *Office Space Planning: Designing for Tomorrow's Workplace.*

Office space is treated by many organizations as a commodity, needing little adaptation to meet the unique attributes of the company. The corporate real estate VP or facility manager selects ready-made space from a serviced office company or a speculative property developer, much as a new car or a new printer might be purchased. Standard monochrome cubicles are ordered from a building interiors contractor or major furniture manufacturer. Furniture is bought from a mail-order supplier and delivered, together with copy paper and printer cartridges. The outcome is formulaic. People "lift and shift" into the new space and carry on just as before. No one has realized that more is possible.

By contrast, other organizations seek the right and valid office space for their needs. They treat office space as an important lever to reinvent customer service, work processes, and behaviors through spatial redesign. They want to change; the new work environment is imagined, then implemented and, in turn, helps drive change.

In fact, this process is a powerful spur to business change. Building changes take months to years, from drawn solution to move-in—enough time for change management on several fronts. Conversely, the overt visibility of new physical space helps to speed up change that might otherwise have happened more slowly.

When people come together in space and time, great things can happen. Yet too many office spaces breed boredom, inefficiency, and anomie; too many museums are user-unfriendly; too many schools turn people away from learning; too many hospitals breed infection; and too many cities are dysfunctional.

Converting poor environments into success stories is never easy. The successful examples work only when a series of necessary steps are followed: the goals and objectives are articulated clearly; top management buys in; physical and process changes go hand in hand; and change is introduced gradually, persistently, and eventually embraced by all.

Physical change without organizational redesign is a lost opportunity. Organizational change without changes to the physical environment is difficult and slow. Physical and organizational redesign together can help reshape our companies, our public institutions, and our urban communities. Most of the time, a "lift and shift" approach to the future is all that is asked. But if clients want "business as usual" to become "business as unusual," then integrating physical and organizational redesign is essential.

RICHARD SWETT

Best known as a former U.S. ambassador and congressman, Richard Swett is also an architect, a senior fellow of the Design Futures Council, a senior counselor at the strategic communication and public relations firm APCO Worldwide, and a senior advisor at the Greenway Group, a consulting firm for the design industry. He's the author of the book *Leadership by Design: Creating an Architecture of Trust.*

Design's absence in many of the professions of today can be traced to two basic facts. First, education, particularly in the U.S., does not teach an appreciation of the design process, much less its utilization as a problem-solving tool. Second, many designers have little desire to apply their skill set to the world outside of design. These two conditions successfully keep the full benefits of design from the broader world of corporate or public governance.

I have seen communities where crossovers have been made to the benefit of both sides, but they are still few and far between. My experience as the American Ambassador to Denmark exposed me to a community that both teaches its youth an appreciation of design and employs the design process consistently in corporate and public problem-solving processes.

I argue that designers must become leaders who bridge the gap between their world and the worlds of commerce and politics because, without the educational preparation in design that is lacking in so many countries, no one is looking for the help design has to offer.

Master builders of yore understood the depth and breadth of society and how design addressed a multitude of issues. We lack this kind of integrated leadership today and although, in the United States, our cities have been built and filled, they must now contend with overcrowding, rehabilitation, renovation, security, and sustainability, to name but a few issues. These are issues that need to be managed by someone with a master builder's eye.

Leaders of today's corporate world come out of an education based on case study. Lawyers share the same experience. In the political world many leaders are the offspring of special interest groups and come to positions of power limited by a narrow vision. The threats to the world can only be solved by an inclusive leadership that integrates all facets of the global community to work harmoniously toward finding solutions. On the economic, environmental, and health fronts business is going to play an important role and will require the vision of the master builder possessed by the designer. Therefore, leadership by design is a must.

ROGER MARTIN

As Dean of the Rotman School of Management and former director of
Monitor Company, a global strategy consulting firm, Roger Martin's research
focuses on global competitiveness, integrative thinking, business design and
corporate citizenship. He's a regular contributor to BusinessWeek Online's
Innovation and Design Channel and has authored three books, his most
recent being *The Future of the MBA: Designing the Thinker of the Future.*

A fundamental difference exists between designers and executives that is poorly understood by both sides, but sometimes drives all involved to engage in behaviors that make the other side nervous and worried. That difference can be seen as a trust in reliability on the one hand, and a search for validity on the other. Every organization faces this tension whether they realize it or not. And if they are not cognizant of it, they could inadvertently crowd out the very innovation and creativity necessary to survive and prosper.

Reliable processes are intended to produce identical or consistent results under all circumstances, primarily by analyzing objective data from the past. For instance, a perfectly reliable poll would produce the same result from 10 random samples of voters. By contrast, a perfectly valid poll would be able to predict an election's winner. A reliable process—which tends to attract folks in finance, engineering, and operations—is business as algorithm: quantifiable, measurable, and provable. It hews to the old management adage, "What doesn't get measured, doesn't get done." A valid process, on the other hand, flows from designers' deep understanding of both user and context, and leads them to ideas they believe in but can't prove. Designers work in a world of variables: the unpredictable, the visual, the experimental, and worry less about replicating a successful process than about producing a spectacular solution.

As the computer scientist Alan Kay put it so memorably, "The best way to predict the future is to invent it." And that is what design-centric organizations do: they peer into the needs and desires of their customers, identify patterns of behavior, refine ideas that tap into those behaviors, then push into the unknown—or at least the uncertain. For example, before John Mackey launched one of the country's first supermarket-style natural-food stores, nobody could prove that Whole Foods Market would succeed at all, let alone become the most profitable food retailer (in terms of profit per square foot) in the United States. But Mackey did it anyway.

An organization that produces reliable, predictable but meaningless results is not unlike a well-tuned car that runs full speed off a cliff. To save themselves, organizations will have to figure out how to be welcoming homes for people who are comfortable handling fuzzy data and using their judgment. Boards must get used to approving plans based on the logic of what might be rather than on regressions of what has always been. James March, the management theorist, believes that by focusing on the intuitive and experiential, organizations can explore new sources of competitive advantage. By looking to the provable and replicable, organizations can better exploit the innovations they've brought to market. And to prosper over the long run, they need to succeed at both. Designers should see their roles as assisting the organizations that they serve to better balance the tension between reliability and validity. The biggest challenge for all of us, designers and business—people alike, is to become equally adept at quantifying the now and intuiting what's next.

ASTRID PUJARI

A board-certified internist and European-trained medical herbalist, Dr. Pujari worked as a primary care physician before starting her clinic, the Pujari Center, in Seattle, Washington. She has a strong interest in the spiritual aspects of health and well being, and in integrating conventional, holistic, and mind-body medicine into a single paradigm for patients. Dr. Pujari is a consultant at the Cancer Institute at Seattle's Virginia Mason hospital.

How do you design for health? Many people define health as the absence of disease. "Get rid of this knee pain and high cholesterol, I'll be healthy again." But defining health as an absence is like defining an orange by saying, "not a gorilla." So how do we define health in positive terms?

Most of us would agree that health in the positive equates with a body that works well. But we all know that there is much more to health than just our physical functioning. Just take someone with depression. We wouldn't say they were healthy, despite good physical shape. In my experience, people with depression have a whole host of feelings. They feel isolated, unlovable, and like failures. They have no energy, and wonder, "What's the point?" Health in the positive, using their experience, equates with a sense of joy, love, connection, empowerment, meaning, vitality and passion.

Let's stop here and look at the simple, two-part definition of health we have come up with. Health is good physical functioning and a sense of joy, love, connection, empowerment, meaning, vitality, and passion. Interestingly, when I ask people what they care most about, they tell me they want a sense of connection, meaning, and joy. Good physical functioning matters less. Strangely, though, in conventional medicine, we spend most of our time trying to achieve good physical functioning. The same happens in architecture when function is emphasized over the human experience of a place.

Many people believe that by achieving good physical functioning, they will achieve joy. Or that if they stop being sad, they will be happy. In my experience, there is a long way between getting to neutral and joy. Happiness doesn't happen by accident. It happens by design. So, if we care most about having a sense of connection, love and meaning in our lives, how do we design a means to get there? For me, the answer is through spirituality.

A lot of people equate spirituality with religion. For me, spirituality is a process by which we take each of the core concepts above—connection, empowerment, meaning—and turn them into questions: "When have I felt a sense of connection in my life? How can I cultivate more of that feeling in the future? What brings me a sense of meaning? Am I living a life that helps or detracts from that? How well do I give and receive love?" We then answer those questions for ourselves, with our lives. Living a life by design takes vision, intention, and a lot of taxing work. But the personal payoff is correspondingly bigger too.

Spirituality is a practice, not a goal. You don't get to peace one day, and then stay there the rest of your life. You live into it, day by day and hour by hour. You need to choose it, again and again. And as you do, you grow something powerful within yourself that contains its own momentum which deepens you and enriches your life experience.

Joyful, inspired, passionate people don't happen by accident. Neither do inspirational, connected, living buildings. These are created when we pay attention first to what matters most—core values. If we jump to the physical before asking ourselves, "Why are we here?" we are going to miss some very key points, if not the entire boat. Physical structures—whether bodies or buildings—function best when we pay attention to what's happening inside. The reward when we do is a living, positive, powerful force which can change the world.

CHANGE DESIGN TOOLS

To help clients use design to encourage and accomplish change, NBBJ has developed and adopted certain methods, or tools, that are not part of the traditional design tool box. NBBJ has discovered that by using these "change tools" in concert with the design tools, it is possible to design buildings that transform the way enterprises of all sorts work. This section of the book collects together the Change Tools used on the projects documented in the Change Design Conversations.

The tools are organized here into four categories: Vision tools help determine the right thing to do; Collaboration tools build common ground, enabling people to better work together; Communication tools aid in establishing a shared understanding; and Delivery tools enable people to realize their vision.

Within those categories, each of the individual tools has a specific goal; it also acts as a framework to be customized for the client and the circumstance. Anecdotes demonstrate how Change Tools enable design teams to address change across multiple dimensions: behavioral, relational, organizational, and performance-related. For detailed examples of how these tools work, flip back to the pages noted at the bottom of each tool description and read an NBBJ designer's account of the tool in action.

CATEGORY:
Vision

GOAL:
Incorporating the vision every step of the way.

KEEP YOUR EYES ON THE PRIZE

Look up from the dailies. Focus on the big picture.

Find a way, any way that works, to remind yourself why you're doing a project and who's going to benefit.

Tying the built environment to your vision makes it a strategic asset rather than merely a commodity. In the drive to get things done, vision can get lost. Constantly and consciously keep vision at the forefront by integrating it into the rhythm of a project. Integrate the vision as a header into meeting notes as a regular reminder of where you're heading and why. The essence of the vision should be ever-present in the team space, both physically and virtually. Given the duration of major projects, we all benefit from keeping the vision constantly in sight.

ON TELENOR, KEEP YOUR EYES ON THE PRIZE PRODUCES A PLAZA THAT DEFINES THE CAMPUS, THE COMPANY, AND THE CULTURE

As you approach the campus, or see it from the fjord, it looks like a hill town. It's not an iconic building from the outside, purposefully. It looks and acts like an assemblage of little buildings, spaces, offices, and courtyards—a community.

You discover the expression of their vision inside. It's the big plaza. Significant plazas have always been significant historically. In Norway they're important spaces because Norwegians love to be outside, due to the long, dark winters. There are more outdoor seats in Oslo's restaurants, per capita, than in any other city of the world. They celebrate being outside.

So the expression and organization, rather than being outward facing and of a singular nature, is of two embracing, sweeping arms that form a central courtyard encouraging interaction and exchange.

BILL NICHOLS, PARTNER, NBBJ

CATEGORY:
Vision

GOAL:
Gaining new insights and discarding tired conventions.

TOOL IN ACTION:
See how this tool vaulted past incremental improvements on Southwest Washington Medical Center.

Page 140

CHALLENGE ASSUMPTIONS

Be six years old again. Ask "Why?" until you're satisfied.

Ask obvious questions, even questions that might seem dumb, like "Why are we doing this?" "Why do it this way?" "What is this space for and why?" Then discard conventional answers. Free from the restraints of old definitions, you're open to do what hasn't been done before.

Assumptions can be deadly in any business. It's difficult to look past long-held success to see something truly new, but asking first questions again is essential for everyone—especially experts.

The best way to elicit new definitions is to create a trust-based environment. If "Can we look at this another way?" is treated as a useless question, the process has been hobbled.

Information is power. Overly broad or familiar definitions limit the information you can access. In order to make an organization different and stronger, you first must be able to see it differently.

ON CALIT2, CHALLENGE ASSUMPTIONS GENERATES A FAÇADE MATERIAL THAT IS AS HIGH TECH AS IT LOOKS

From the start, this was supposed to be a very technical-looking building. The original idea was to have a metal panel system that would express the desire for a very high-tech, modern look, while being very economical and reliable. The difficulty was that a metal exterior cladding system would shut down the radio signals coming through all of the building's wireless locations. We challenged the idea of a metal system being the only or best way to express their goal of a technological expression by doing further research. We found a panel system which is a wood fiber-based plastic. It looks very high-tech, but it's transparent to radio frequencies. So, as far as expressing technology, the big opaque exterior walls are actually the most transparent, and the glass walls with aluminum mullions are the least transparent. This contradiction of the initial assumptions took a little getting used to.

FRED POWELL, SENIOR ASSOCIATE, NBBJ

CATEGORY:
Vision

GOAL:
Tying need to vision.

TOOL IN ACTION:
See how this tool kept the transformation of Boeing's Renton site on course.

Page 64

LET VISION DRIVE THE PROGRAMMING

Put the spreadsheets away for a minute and ask, "What is it we really want to accomplish? Not just now, but far from now."

Go beyond what you think the project limits are. "Programming"—the first phase of designing a building—identifies space requirements, develops critical functional adjacencies, tests layouts and "process flow" alternatives. Programming typically makes the building's first use the highest priority. Since companies change faster than ever, first use can equal obsolescence at move-in.

Programming can be used for more than measuring projected headcount and cataloging equipment, technology, and space needs. "Enhanced programming" helps get to the heart of a company's vision and operations by assessing behavior, work patterns, future goals and trends alongside practical space needs. In this way, program goals tie needs to the vision, targeting proactive change and capturing performance metrics across organizational and environmental measures.

Expand the boundaries of the challenge. Make the problem bigger than you initially think it is and you'll solve the root cause instead of simply addressing the symptom.

ON BANNER ESTRELLA, LET VISION DRIVE THE PROGRAMMING ALLOWS A CONFERENCE OF THOUGHT LEADERS TO INFORM THE PROJECT

We invited visionaries and leaders from healthcare institutions across the nation and asked them to speak to us about the future of healthcare: What should the hospital of the future be? What kind of services would be provided and what kind of issues are going to be important? What role does technology play in this and how do the humanitarian issues play into this kind of delivery? This exercise got us beyond the tyranny of designing and programming for first use—for the present only.

JOHN PANGRAZIO, PARTNER, NBBJ

ON UNIVERSITY OF WASHINGTON BOTHELL, LET VISION DRIVE THE PROGRAMMING FOCUSES ON AN ICON OF CO-LOCATION

One of the factors in all of the plans that were made was this tree. It's a great old maple, and it stands on a little slope. There was a farmhouse, and the maple was in the front yard. And everybody would say, "There's no way we can keep that grand old tree because there's too much program to fit in there." So the secret little challenge for the design team was: we're going to save that tree, and it's going to become special.

When the project moved, finally, to the idea of the lineal campus, the tree became part of the retained space. And during the construction of the campus, as proof of the attractiveness of this one grand old tree that most people would have taken out years ago, the contractors, these tough guys in these big machines, would shut off their big machines and climb this dusty little hill, and they'd all gather under this maple and have their lunch. And on the day the campus opened, the first day of classes, there was an instructor talking to this class of about 40 guys and girls—all sitting under the maple tree.

BILL JOHNSON, NBBJ

CATEGORY:
Vision / Communication

GOAL:
Establishing systems that bring order to chaos.

SEE THIS TOOL IN ACTION:
See how this tool helped identify, represent, and design for Telenor's collaborative structures.

Page 15

SIMPLIFY COMPLEXITY

Search for patterns and be ready to recognize them. They will simplify your life and your work.

Copernicus, Newton, and Darwin found patterns in the world that accelerated discovery. Complex, multifaceted situations can often seem chaotic and contradictory. Pattern recognition opens a direct route to simplicity and solution, releasing capacity that would otherwise be tied up in pursuit of needless complication. Actively pursue the moments when patterns materialize.

Think of patterns as catalysts for understanding systems. Recognizing patterns of use, flow, and change, all functioning at multiple scales, helps us to clarify our place in the world as individuals and, as an organization, to develop an appropriate and useful response. Long-range forecasting is one such method by which an organization's recognition of patterns is used to plot strategy and action.

By recognizing patterns of use, you can discover what is relatively permanent (long cycles of change) and what is adaptable (short cycles of change). This helps to determine long-term investment and short-term placement of expensive building infrastructure. In turn, you can identify elements that need the highest level of detail and how they might relate to a unified whole.

ON SOUTHWEST WASHINGTON MEDICAL CENTER, SIMPLIFY COMPLEXITY SHAPES A NEW TEMPLATE FOR PATIENT ROOMS

The SWMC leadership wanted to increase patient and staff safety in the design of the patient room, and create an environment that would help speed up the healing process. The industry norm, at the time, was mirrored patient room layouts where every room was arranged in reverse to the one next to it. So when a doctor or nurse would walk in they would have to mentally and physically adjust to the right-handed- or left-handedness of a room, which was inefficient and allowed more room for error in the care-giving process.

We looked at research done on industrial processes and lean principles where efficiency and flow are enhanced by streamlining actions that create value and eliminating those that don't. We thought, why not eliminate that readjustment period for clinical staff by making all patient rooms same-handed, so equipment, supplies and furniture are laid out in the exact same manner. An oxygen line on the left side is always on the left side in every single patient room. This would increase safety by eliminating wasted time and reducing errors, and provide a more efficient standard work environment for delivering care.

We also included several features that provide the patient with greater connection to the outdoors and to their caregivers, allow ease of movement throughout the space, and maximize comfort for the patient and family.

LYNNE SHIRA, PRINCIPAL, NBBJ

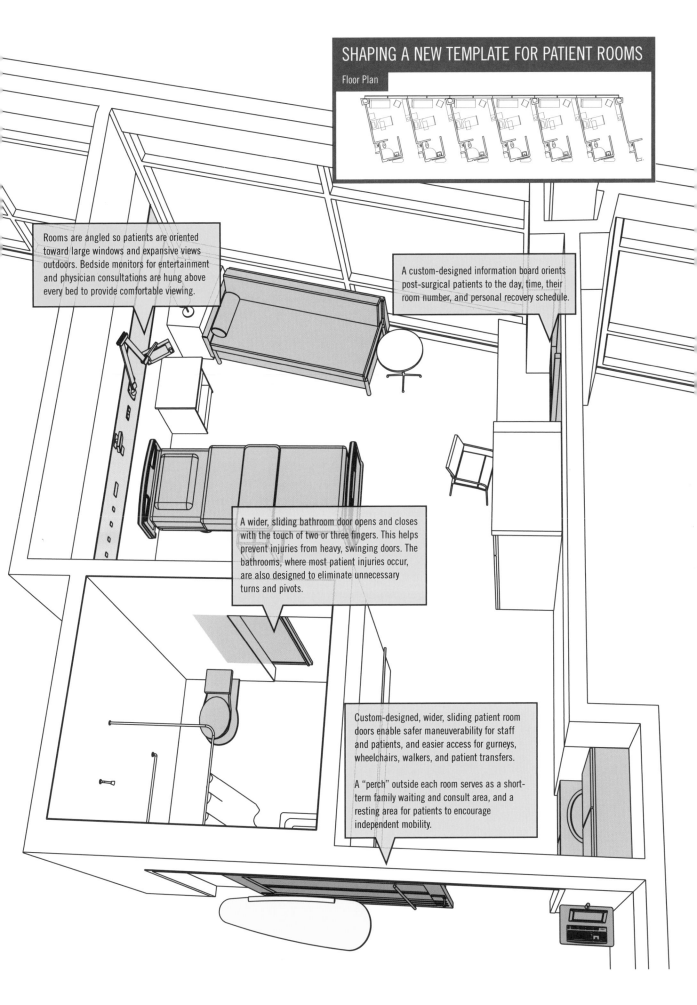

SHAPING A NEW TEMPLATE FOR PATIENT ROOMS

Floor Plan

Rooms are angled so patients are oriented toward large windows and expansive views outdoors. Bedside monitors for entertainment and physician consultations are hung above every bed to provide comfortable viewing.

A custom-designed information board orients post-surgical patients to the day, time, their room number, and personal recovery schedule.

A wider, sliding bathroom door opens and closes with the touch of two or three fingers. This helps prevent injuries from heavy, swinging doors. The bathrooms, where most patient injuries occur, are also designed to eliminate unnecessary turns and pivots.

Custom-designed, wider, sliding patient room doors enable safer maneuverability for staff and patients, and easier access for gurneys, wheelchairs, walkers, and patient transfers.

A "perch" outside each room serves as a short-term family waiting and consult area, and a resting area for patients to encourage independent mobility.

CATEGORY:
Vision / Communication

GOAL:
Broaden your vision.

TOOL IN ACTION:
See how this tool transformed Banner Estrella into a unique healing environment.

Page 29

See how this tool provoked contextual thinking and a better environment for all on Bothell.

Page 104

SITE SEE

Step outside. Look past your immediate boundaries to see what's possible.

Go beyond the organization to make critical observations about your place at all scales—the immediate site, neighborhood, city, state, country, world. Uncover potential opportunities, identify constraints, and unearth secrets. Look at how and where people move and gather. Look at streets, dynamic densities, defined spaces, diversity, history, compactness, or distinctive character.

Big ideas come from big picture viewpoints, and from the small things as well. Search for the unique physical and experiential characteristics of a site. This contextual thinking will contribute to better environments for people.

By cataloging and connecting diverse site influences, Site Seeing is a tool that provokes visionary thinking. Inspiration from these observations can transform a location into a special place by adding content, meaning, and values.

ON ALLEY24, SITE SEE PICKS UP URBAN CUES TO TRANSFORM AN INDUSTRIAL SITE INTO A PUBLIC SPACE

When we were considering the potential of the Richmond Laundry site in South Lake Union—that's what Alley24 was originally called—the first thing we explored was the urban fabric of the neighborhood. There's a very dominant north/south connection between Lake Union and downtown Seattle, which creates a street pattern in the area of long rectangular city blocks. That grid inspired the project's cross-block alleys. It also eventually gave the project its name. But there was more to this move than mimicking the city grid. In urban areas where there's a shortage of public parks, streets and alleys become the public spaces. They bring a usefulness and a human scale to the urban experience that's really important. So we were looking beyond the functionality of the alley—we wanted it to bring new life to the area, and contribute to the city's open space.

VINCE VERGEL DE DIOS, PRINCIPAL, NBBJ

We also took cues from three historic buildings on the site—the buildings that had at one time belonged to the Richmond Laundry. We re-used parts of the buildings, which maintained the site's historic identity and scale. Other parts we removed, to create the east-west, through-block connection. We interwove the new and the historic. We mixed commercial, residential, and retail on one block. And, by locating office and residential entrances inside the block, we drove pedestrian traffic through the alleyways. All of this created a really lively, pedestrian-oriented space. It has an urban coherence, and it's a safe and pleasant place to be.

BRENT ROGERS, PRINCIPAL, NBBJ

ON WELLCOME TRUST, SITE SEE ESTABLISHES A BUILDING APPROACH THAT ADDRESSES ENVIRONMENTAL AND SOCIAL NEEDS

The site is extremely delicate. The Cambridgeshire environment is mostly agricultural; Cambridge itself is a 20-minute drive away. There are other developments, including laboratories being built in the countryside, and there's a lot of concern from the local villages to slow down the spread of development and not let it completely change the landscape. The design team took that as a cue and asked: "What can we do to make this building fit onto the site?" It's a very open site; you can see it from far away because it's flat. There are hills surrounding one side and a small village on the other side. The team spent a lot of time talking about the concept of cutting into the landscape and slipping the building into those cuts, so the landscape would mask the very technical parts of the building. We wanted the people parts to be as open as possible, but as you moved away from that you could start digging into the earth, blocking the bulk of the building from view from the village.

JONATHAN WARD, PARTNER, NBBJ

CATEGORY:
Vision / Delivery

GOAL:
Enabling the catalysts of change.

WORK WITH CHANGE AGENTS

Change. You can fight it and fail or embrace it and flourish.

Change agents are pathfinders who move us forward. They are the ones who recognize the future and know how to get there. Find the change agents in your organization and get them on board.

Change agents have the vision and skills to create a new "social architecture" as the basis of your organization's network.

Put a change agent on your design team. Change agents see the enterprise in terms of assets to be leveraged. When it comes to the design of new environments, they see opportunities to change work patterns and behaviors and to link new business processes and systems with facilities.

Since change agents often occupy the "in between" space within an enterprise, they see the world from a unique perspective. Harness their insights and possibilities will multiply.

Change agents focus less on specific goals and more on organizational readiness. Rather than aiming for straightforward growth, change agents aim for agility.

ON BOEING, WORK WITH CHANGE AGENTS DRIVES THE REDESIGN OF A WORKPLACE AND A WORK CULTURE

Within every large organization is a mix of people with differing perspectives and opinions. Their perceived objectives within the organization can sometimes be seen as divergent. This is one reason change can be so difficult. Boeing's Commercial Airlines Division had a leader with a clear vision of what she was trying to accomplish with this project. This vision, its conceptualization, the drive to be more efficient by bringing the mechanics and engineers together, came from her division. The design team's job was to work with her and her division as the primary agents of change and other entities within Boeing to achieve a win-win solution for all stakeholders.

LORI WALKER, PRINCIPAL, NBBJ

CATEGORY:
Vision

GOAL:
Developing a critical mass of support for change.

TOOL IN ACTION:
See how this tool engaged Southwest Washington Medical Center's external customers and internal clients.

Page 140

CREATE CHAMPIONS FOR THE VISION

It's hard to realize a vision by yourself. It requires a critical mass of dedicated leaders at all levels within an enterprise. They must work across disciplinary boundaries to help people realize that the change required to achieve a vision is worth it.

Change is constant and often difficult. Change happens from the inside out, and from the outside in. It often requires behavioral change. Vision gives us inspiration and hope.

Identify key opinion leaders in the organization who support your enterprise vision and put them inside the change process. They'll help to spread the word. Their actions will foster an appropriate balance between vision and the daily activities required to get us there. As role models for those who follow, they play an important role in successfully launching a new paradigm and realizing a vision.

ON BANNER ESTRELLA, CREATE CHAMPIONS FOR THE VISION ENLISTS BROAD SUPPORT FOR A NEW MODEL OF HEALTHCARE

Banner Estrella's vision was about reorganizing the hospital delivery organization to shift it to a more collaborative culture, reduce redundancy, share resources, and improve patient safety. This would require a level of behavioral change beyond what designers and administrators could mandate. It meant a change in the cultural currency of the traditional healthcare organization.

MACKENZIE SKENE, PARTNER, NBBJ

Banner's leadership enlisted key physicians and administrators, people who believed in the potential of reorganization. They became the enablers of a new practice vision. These were people who didn't wait for a "green light." They stepped right up to address naysayers. They provided clarification and responded to objections. They propelled the ideas about the merits of the model through all levels of the organization. It was these people who breathed life into the vision, gave it legs and purpose. Without their talents and purposefulness, Banner Estrella would never have been realized.

CHARLES MARTIN, PRINCIPAL, NBBJ

CATEGORY:
Collaboration

GOAL:
Building trust
and common understanding.

BREAK BREAD

Turn off the meter and pull over for a bite to eat.

Shed the trappings of professionalism—the client/consultant divide—and meet as people.

Changing the context for communication brings out diverse viewpoints that otherwise are left unsaid and thus unheard. Sharing a meal—away from the typical meeting structure—allows behavior to relax and perspectives to shift. When people sit and eat with each other they learn about life and each other, and build common ground.

The civilizing influence of that most basic of social structures, the meal, builds bridges and creates social networks that carry you forward. And when the inevitable difficult moments arise, the bonds and common understanding built in this simple but effective way help bring people together to resolve their differences.

ON UNIVERSITY OF WASHINGTON BOTHELL, BREAK BREAD TURNS DISPUTED TERRITORY INTO COMMON GROUND

Once a month, NBBJ held a stakeholders meeting that ran through the evening. During these meetings there would be all this fighting, arguing, sometimes even yelling, and then people had to sit down and share a meal. It was like a family—there's an argument, but you sit down and eat dinner together.

LIZ JACKS, PRINCIPAL, NBBJ

The value of breaking bread—coming together with food to discuss ongoing challenges—was a civilizing influence that changed the context for communication and created common ground. When the plan went through the final environmental review, when it went through the city process for approval, when it went through the federal process for approvals—approvals were gained in record time with very little formal opposition.

BILL SANFORD, PARTNER, NBBJ

CATEGORY:
Collaboration

GOAL:
Human-centered design begins
with human relationships.

DESIGN THE RELATIONSHIP

It's a long ride. Know who you're driving with before you hit the road.

Before you begin the business of designing places, processes, and human experiences, start with each other. Articulate and understand personal and organizational values. Discover preferences for communication.

Before designing an environment, begin by designing the relationships with critical constituencies. Go beyond mirroring seniority levels to understand how to engage most effectively, both individually and collectively.

Understanding one another as people, knowing what we fundamentally value, enables us to move past the transactional. It frees us to address what is transformational. The environments we invest in are no longer mere commodities, but express deeply rooted aspirations.

How do you design the relationship? There are many ways. Focused Site Seeing builds relationships while deepening relevant knowledge. Off-site team-building retreats scheduled at the beginning of a project and at key milestones throughout the process build relationships and ensure that time for relationship building is a continuing priority.

Asking a physician why he originally went into medicine moves the conversation past the necessary and expected questions of medical delivery to questions of root cause. It reveals a fundamental belief in the healing power of nature and the design responds by integrating garden spaces throughout a medical environment.

Insights like this change our understanding of how the design of environments can inspire and transform us.

ON UNIVERSITY OF WASHINGTON BOTHELL, DESIGN THE RELATIONSHIP BUILDS TRUST, FAITH, AND A NEW CAMPUS

Initially, all the stakeholders in the Bothell project, particularly the institutions, saw co-location as an arranged marriage driven by the state legislature. There was no consensus on the value of the project and little trust in its success.

We began building trust by asking stakeholders a question about success: "It is as good as it gets when...?" Out of the answers they understood each other's hopes and fears. A common vision emerged about education, community and environmental and economic sustainability. Building on this, we began to "design" a new campus together. This process illustrated that there was no hidden agenda.

The relationships and the process became intertwined. The analytical rigor we went through ultimately turned antagonists into advocates. Content got us to common ground, got us approvals in half the normal time, and allowed us to meet the mandated campus opening date.

BILL SANFORD, PARTNER, NBBJ

CATEGORY:
Collaboration

GOAL:
Broadening perspectives.

INVEST IN TRAVEL

Pack your bags and hit the road.

Become anthropologists. Together. Explore the way others inside and outside your field innovate with their processes and environments—even if it requires travel to a faraway country.

By taking field trips, you gain social proof that can be leveraged in support of new ideas. Look for examples of solutions that have worked in parallel situations. Study people's activities in these environments and note the relationship between places and activities. Discuss how the environments you visit impact people's work lives, habits, and values. Talk to the people least likely to be asked their opinion. Document vigorously.

The journey provides context and background research for shared discovery, leading to the development of a project's vision. It helps connect everyone to a common experience that binds a team together.

ON WELLCOME TRUST, INVEST IN TRAVEL DELIVERS EVIDENCE AND CONFIDENCE IN DESIGN SOLUTIONS

John Cooper asked the team what the riskiest part of the project was. "Well, the riskiest part of this project is the data center, because it has to stay live, and it's big and it's powerful." It's well above normal design criteria. The team was talking about going to look at some new cooling systems in the United States, and John Cooper said, "If you guys think this is risky, we'd better get out there, go visit them and make sure we know what we're getting ourselves into."

BRUCE NEPP, PRINCIPAL, NBBJ

ON ALLEY24, INVEST IN TRAVEL PROVIDES BEST PRACTICES FOR SUSTAINABLE RE-USE OF HISTORIC BUILDINGS

Alley24's owners, contractor, and design team traveled to Stockholm, Sweden, and to the historic Pearl District in Portland, Oregon, to look at urban design and sustainable solutions. In Stockholm, we saw how progressive European projects approach sustainability and how they reuse existing building stock, and their best practices informed our approach to Alley24. Both of the trips also reinforced how important it is to create a really rich and diverse urban experience—and how critical it is to have an environment that's safe for pedestrians.

BRENT ROGERS, PRINCIPAL, NBBJ

ON THE SEATTLE COURTHOUSE, INVEST IN TRAVEL YIELDS JOINT UNDERSTANDING OF BEST PRACTICES

One thing about touring is that it's important to be focused, so the team identified sites ahead of time, such as the John Joseph Moakley United States Courthouse in Boston, Massachusetts, designed by Pei Cobb Freed & Partners Architects LLP and shown here. Each site was included for a particular reason: one for technology integration, another for aesthetics. The team targeted why they were going to a site, what they were looking at, and what they were looking to understand, so a lot was learned. Of course, touring with clients is one of the best ways to have the entire team focus, to learn a common language, and create a common reference. So the tour was an important building block in making a quality collaboration with the judges.

BILL BAIN, PARTNER, NBBJ

CATEGORY:
Collaboration

GOAL:
Ensuring that the best idea wins.

MAKE EVERYONE THE ARCHITECT

You never know who will have the best idea. So ask.

Invite people to the table who aren't typically involved in design—people from a diverse range of activities within your enterprise whose experiences enable a broader understanding of behavior and flow. Including them at the design table allows their insights to have a direct impact on idea generation. Let a receptionist design the waiting areas. Ask transporters to design the corridor system. Invite hospital inpatients to design their room and the gowns they'll wear. Their solutions will both surprise and amaze you.

There are hidden experts waiting to get involved. When asked, they deliver real value.

ON BANNER ESTRELLA, MAKE EVERYONE THE ARCHITECT SEEDS THE IDEA OF A PROTOTYPE HOSPITAL

As part of the visioning sessions, we invited about 150 people, mostly Banner employees or representatives from the community. We broke down into groups and each group included an architect from the design team. The groups spent two to three hours building a model from a kit of parts of what they felt the vision of the hospital for the future should be.

JOHN PANGRAZIO, PARTNER, NBBJ

Some teams tried to build as best they could and some did more abstract solutions that mirrored what they felt were the key issues. All the groups came to the conclusion that the hospital of the future is very different than what they had been building or what they had at present.

At the end, they said, "We need to develop Banner as a system; we need to develop a prototype of a hospital that becomes a platform, if not a chassis, to beta test various issues and innovations."

SCOTT DUNLAP, SENIOR ASSOCIATE, NBBJ

ON BOEING, MAKE EVERYONE THE ARCHITECT LINKS PEOPLE, PRODUCT, AND DESIGN

Boeing Surplus is a vast warehouse of leftovers from the factories, open to the public. The unexpected array, such as abandoned bamboo crates used for shipping airplane parts, makes a wonderful creative outlet. Seeing this lovely woven material in a different context was our genesis for incorporating Boeing products into the design.

We moved some huge templates from which airplane parts had been cut onto the site and began compositional studies. Boeing painters joined us first and then others on the floor got inspired. We provided guidelines and let them go for it. The "moonshine people" who work the two night shifts began doing really interesting pieces. All the artwork created became a design metaphor for our vision, "Parts to Whole."

ERIC LEVINE, PRINCIPAL, NBBJ

CATEGORY:
Collaboration

GOAL:
Integrating diverse intelligence yields greater opportunity for high-performance outcomes.

TOOL IN ACTION:
See how this tool brought in the skills to burrow deeper and wider into the Southwest Washington Medical Center client experience.

Page 140

See how this tool prompted the Calit2 team to use multiple lenses to see through complex problems.

Page 161

BUILD RENAISSANCE TEAMS

Socrates was right. Dialogue is always more productive.

Given the sheer amount of and ready access to data and information in today's world it is no longer possible to be a Renaissance man or woman. So, rather than looking for the solitary genius, build Renaissance teams.

The most enlightened ideas start with the coming together of diverse perspectives. Include people who are broad and generous in their desire to work with others while having a depth of individual talent that adds color and breadth to your team. By integrating a variety of fully engaged talent from the start, you increase your chances of producing high-performance outcomes with lasting meaning.

Like-minded people have a tendency to develop like-minded solutions. This can lead to blind spots in process, ideation, and delivery. Renaissance teams help us individually break through the barriers of our training and ingrained processes.

When confronted with complex challenges, Renaissance teams see the challenges through multiple lenses. That increases their opportunity to develop a wider range of ideas with greater density of thought and action.

GIVE CLIENTS THE KEYS

Move over and let someone else drive. There's nothing like the view from the driver's seat to help clarify where you're going.

Give clients the metaphorical keys to your car and let them know they're welcome to drive any time. Invite them into your process. Expose them to your tools and teach their use. Make it clear from the beginning that the solution is just as likely to come from them as it is from you, especially when shifting to a new paradigm.

When clients are co-designers, everyone owns the results, and the benefits to the larger enterprise are explicit.

CATEGORY:
Collaboration

GOAL:
Being open to and soliciting alternative points of view.

ON CALIT2, GIVE CLIENTS THE KEYS FOCUSES THE DESIGN PROCESS ON VALUE ADDED

Any environment designed to integrate and develop the highest technology, whether it's a medical, research, or educational facility, will change—repeatedly—and fast. Calit2's focus is on the future of the Internet. They recognize that this requires diverse, integrated intelligence. Mirroring their vision of a persistent collaborative framework, we invited the client in as a co-designer. Sitting side by side from the beginning, we developed performance criteria for the building systems that would enable rapid change and a series of alternative concepts for how those systems could be realized. This was an important first step because we collectively realized that these systems would drive the cost of the building now and into the future. We immediately understood the price tag for different levels of flexibility and could assess value to refine and further develop concepts. By doing this together, we avoided the typical iterative, non-value-added process where experts present ideas to the client. It's easier to make tough, informed choices when you're in the driver's seat.

BRAD LEATHLEY, PRINCIPAL, NBBJ

CATEGORY:
Vision / Collaboration

GOAL:
Understanding the intersections of human experience and the built environment.

TOOL IN ACTION:
See how this tool led to new understandings about NBBJ's own workforce and patterns of activity on Alley24.

Page 50

See how this tool enabled Southwest Washington Medical Center to meet the needs of both its external customers and its internal clients.

Page 140

EXPLORE THE EXPERIENCE

Take the time to get to know a client really well by exploring two distinct but converging paths—the business path and the people path. Explore a client's business model, processes, and culture, while delving deeply into the expectations, emotions, patterns, and habits of those who will experience the built environment. Take a hands-on, collaborative approach to developing the discovery process. This leads to a deep understanding of all the stakeholders and builds a firm foundation for creating ideas relevant to current needs and future aspirations. Provide people with opportunities and the tools to express their ideas, and incorporate the expertise and methodologies of market researchers, social scientists, business strategists, architects, and other designers. Sparks happen in the integration of multiple points of view.

Each tool and method for exploration and discovery provides a unique perspective on understanding the intersections of human experience and the built environment. Let each client and their specific needs guide which tools and methods to use. Explore a combination of what people say, what people do, and what people make.

WALK-ALONGS
Rapid touring of a broad range of environments is a useful way to see people in their natural environments. Use it initially to inform and frame the investigation. The note taking and photographic journaling of walk-alongs will be useful later to describe possible future activities for exploration.

THREE-QUESTION INTERVIEWS
Use this simple tool for upfront information gathering. Ask users three fundamental questions to focus their emotions: What was good about your experience today? What could be improved about your experience today? What three words best describe your ideal future experience? Tailor the questions to each client and project.

OBSERVATIONS
Much like an ethnographer, focus on the links between human behavior, culture, and space by spending time in facilities observing people going about their day-to-day activities. Understand what people actually do in addition to what they say they do. See what already happens and let that inspire design.

PARTICIPATORY WORKSHOPS
Participatory design activities engage people creatively by providing them with tool kits designed to provoke their imagination, evoke emotions, and stimulate ideation. These activities can reveal a person's feelings about his/her past and/or desired future, while storytelling can express tacit knowledge and emotional content. Starting with a homework assignment that they bring to the workshop, people work together through a series of exercises to imagine and express their "ideal" experiences for future products, services, or environments.

WALK A MILE IN THEIR SHOES
Take a mock journey based on the actual circumstances of a user and experience what they do and feel. During the journey, have one member of the design team take on the role of the user while the other team member records that person's emotional and physical responses. Evoke empathy with the user by focusing not on the physical qualities of the space, but on how it makes us feel as people.

ON SOUTHWEST WASHINGTON MEDICAL CENTER, EXPLORE THE EXPERIENCE REVEALS THE KEYS TO ENHANCING THE PATIENT EXPERIENCE WITH THE PATIENT ROOM DESIGN

We came up with two big questions for the patients, nurses, and physicians at SWMC. How did they perceive the current patient experience, in positive and negative terms? What did they imagine the future patient experience could look and feel like? We prepared generative tool kits to explore each question.

The first tool kit helped us make a timeline of the current patient experience. We conducted participatory workshops with nurses and physicians and private sessions with patients in SWMC rooms at that time. The timeline revealed the current highs (interactions with the hospital staff) and lows (the noise and the smell).

The second tool kit helped us map out a future patient room. The map revealed that patients need to control environmental factors such as light, temperature, music, communication, and TV. The map also showed that patients feel more like themselves if they can have, in the hospital, books, blanket, pillow, robe and slippers, newspaper, cell phone, hygiene and cosmetic items—the small things they take for granted at home.

LIZ SANDERS, CONSULTANT TO NBBJ/REV

GOAL:
Visualizing, understanding, and coordinating.

MODEL IT

Before you put the shovel in the ground, make sure everyone understands what it is they are getting. This upfront investment will provide a huge payback later, when ribbons are cut.

Two-dimensional drawings are a useful shorthand for planning and construction. However, while most building design professionals are educated to understand the abstraction of this form of graphic communication, the people they serve are not. Most clients have a difficult time fully understanding two-dimensional drawings and are often reluctant to admit it.

Instead, make the communication of ideas and concepts three-dimensional like the world we live in. Use models at all scales to allow people to better imagine, experience, and test the coming reality. Tune the use of models to suit their role as communication, change management, or construction delivery tools. This helps you to arrive at the right solution and save money in the long run.

IDEA MODELS

Rough idea models allow teams to test ideas rapidly. Idea models make the intangible tangible. Palm-sized idea models printed from a 3D printer can be used by teams who need to share concepts on the go. Use these quick studies to develop, test, and critique ideas.

FULL-SCALE PROTOTYPES

Full-scale rough prototypes of complicated environments let people get inside, try on experiences, and "kick the tires." Go beyond plywood and foam core; design the prototype to simulate not just spatial experiences, but sensory experiences as well, such as light, aesthetics, and acoustics. Rigorously observe and record how people use the environment, manipulate elements, and interact with one another when they are in the prototypes.

FULL-SCALE MOCK-UPS

Full-scale mock-ups differ from prototypes since their primary use is as a faithful replica of a completed design for the testing of fit and finish during construction. Mock-ups typically confirm quality expectations and test our understanding of what is to be built.

IMMERSIVE 4D MODELS

When large shifts in the way people work are expected for a move into a new building, use immersive 4D models as powerful change management tools. For large groups, real-time models shown in IMAX-type theater settings offer the closest parallel to physical space. The ability to take employees or members of the public on a "walk-through" builds understanding. Because a 4D model simulates experience, it breeds familiarity, helps eradicate unknowns, and manages the resistance to change.

BUILDING INFORMATION MODELING

Designers and builders now offer new delivery solutions that address the unpredictability and adversarial nature of the traditional design-bid-build process. Building Information Modeling (BIM) creates intelligent digital 3D models instead of paper drawings to communicate design ideas, and guide construction. BIM creates an integrated solution with fewer elements of risk for all parties. Taken to the next level, Building Information Modeling will move toward "Enterprise Information Modeling," where data captured during programming and pre-design will allow for strategic scenario development as it impacts the built environment.

ON TELENOR, IMMERSIVE 4D MODELING MAKES BIG CHANGE FAMILIAR

We built a virtual model of the building not to wow the audience but rather to show people how work can be different. Your office isn't a little place with a door on it anymore, it's the entire building. Throughout the day you will be in meetings in private conference rooms, in open spaces. You'll be in big lecture halls. You'll be at a desk, whichever one is available. You'll be on your cell phone walking through the plaza. That's the workplace.

We put the virtual model in a surround-screen, three-projector, immersive theater that held 25 people at a time. At least five days a week Telenor put staff through. The result was when people first arrived in the new building they knew what to do, they were happy, and it worked. I've seen much, much less change take place with disastrous results because nobody really knew what the change meant.

DUNCAN GRIFFIN, SENIOR ASSOCIATE, NBBJ

ON THE SEATTLE COURTHOUSE, A FULL-SCALE MOCK-UP LETS USERS PERFECT THEIR SPACE

Courtrooms are theatrical environments in the way the faces of witnesses—their stress, the beads of sweat—say something to the jury. When the design team built a full-size mock-up of the courtroom, they hired a stage crew who was knowledgeable about lighting and aesthetics, rather than a contractor to nail up a bunch of plywood. We created an environment that replicated the finished courtroom, but used creative stage-set technology which, as an added bonus, is actually very inexpensive. It served its purpose by engaging the judges, who made subtle adjustments to perfect the space.

JIM TULLY, PRINCIPAL, NBBJ

CATEGORY:
Communication

GOAL:
Learning the client's language.

TOOL IN ACTION:
See how this tool drove the Seattle courthouse team to discover a common, comfortable, and productive language.

Page 127

SPEAK THE RIGHT LANGUAGE

Eschew obfuscation! Leave the jargon at home and learn the language of your client's enterprise.

Every client, industry, or organization has a way of communicating that's all its own. Figure out what those "languages" are. Develop a common language that is comfortable and productive—words, charts, diagrams, images, models, objects... Sometimes, it can even be places or body language. Don't rely on just one language. Being multilingual means you'll have a greater opportunity to communicate and understand.

Early in the design process, as a means of understanding the client's enterprise, ask participants to create a collage that explains a particular process or experience that they feel is important to their enterprise. Have them explain the significance of images chosen. Associating descriptions with different design concepts or features helps people verbalize complex themes. It helps the team evaluate and prioritize design features and concepts. It builds shared understanding and shapes the language of design intent.

When communicating design concepts, explore the use of different "languages" to ensure that people understand the connection between their enterprise and the design. Learn what "language" makes your client most comfortable and use it when you're with them.

CATEGORY:
Communication

GOAL:
Visualizing and understanding
ideas in real time.

DESIGN ON THE FLY

Transcend words. Stop mid-sentence and express an idea visually, right now. You'll be surprised how quickly people really understand what you mean.

Draw, sketch, diagram, and map ideas in real time; involve everyone, not just the designers. Think of problem-solving in hallways, cafes, and mid-meeting as just-in-time design.

When team members talk about ideas and concepts, make it visual on the spot. Everyone can then ask: "Is this what you mean?" for a quick joint grasp of intent.

Real-time sketching resolves problems the moment they occur. It allows the team to rapidly explore, articulate, and visualize design concepts. Sometimes they are simple studies that explore causality—if you want x, it means redesigning y. Other times, they test behaviors—if you're going to work like this in the new environment, it looks like that. Accelerated explorations surface the key aspects of an issue as it relates to the built environment. They move conversations from the abstract to a tangible visual expression of an idea—from problem to solution.

ON WELLCOME TRUST, DESIGN ON THE FLY LETS THE TEAM EVALUATE AND TEST OPTIONS AS THEY EMERGE

We were being asked if Sanger's computing design load was realistic. On our U.S. trip to visit different facilities, talk started among the team in the aisles of the airplane about the growth pattern of the Sanger. How do you justify what you need for the data center? How often will the hardware change?

So the laptops came out and we started quizzing Phil Butcher: "When you started, what was your computer processing load (MIPS)?" We tracked three different historical points, up until the design time in 2002, and came up with logarithmic growth that suggested that within 24 months of opening they could run out of capacity in the data center.

The team came to the realization that the question was "how do you get more capacity?" And of course you could hear John Cooper saying, "You're not spending another penny more."

So we quickly deduced that our only option was the innovative cooling solution, which in turn allowed us to double the computational processing capacity.

BRUCE NEPP, PRINCIPAL, NBBJ

CATEGORY:
Delivery

GOAL:
Creating process clarity and a road map for realizing your vision.

TOOL IN ACTION:
See how this tool was used on Wellcome Trust to identify the project and the organization's guiding principles.

Page 77

DESIGN THE PROCESS

What's the issue? Who's responsible? By when? Let the people involved determine the answers.

Every client challenge, site, and context is unique. That's why it's just as important to design the process for a project as it is to design the project. Managing a creative course of action means building methods and tools that help people collaborate around a shared vision.

Change projects are big, complex journeys into uncharted territory. You need a road map that identifies key milestones. They will keep you on course, guiding your efforts while giving you the freedom to make course corrections along the way.

JAZZ THE PROCESS
We're not just reading sheet music here.

Rather than writing down every note, jazz creates a collectively understood and agreed upon creative framework. It sets themes that allow for and encourage individual variation. Rather than being entirely prescriptive, jazz is a guide, a compass for creativity that anticipates change and adaptability. Jazz acknowledges the reality of constantly changing circumstances and builds in the ability to make adjustments while staying on course.

Design the design process as if you are a jazz ensemble.

There is clearly an element of trust in jazz. A musical framework points everyone in the same direction and creates touchstones that allow the ensemble to monitor their progress. Within this strategic framework, individuals are given a range of freedom to chart their own courses, trusting in each other's talent. In a symphony all eyes are on the conductor. In jazz, all eyes and ears are on each other—watchful, vigilant, ready for change and willing to adapt as the unexpected occurs.

BUILD TOUCHSTONES
A clearly worded mission statement, a short set of guiding principles, story-boards that combine text and images to visually communicate vision, concept, and progress—keep them handy to use whenever decisions come up. They keep your vision accessible, reminding you of where you began and where you are going.

HOLD REGULARLY SCHEDULED MEETINGS TO CONSTANTLY DESIGN THE PROCESS
Hold a session to initiate the design of the ideal process for the project based on your organization, the key stakeholders, and the vision. Inspired minds alone, however prolific, are nothing without processes designed specifically to translate ideas into valuable solutions. Anticipate change by scheduling periodic meetings. Use them to review, update, and change the process to meet changing needs and conditions.

DEFINE EVERYONE'S ROLE
Put everyone's title in a drawer and instead focus on the clarity of each person's role. Assess team talent, interest, and passion to determine who should be responsible for what.

Initiate a meeting to define who owns what. Ask each person to state his or her interests. Then ask each person to state what he or she expects from others— clients, user advocates, architects, engineers, contractors. Explore the intriguing area of expectation that lies outside your own view of what you're "supposed" to do.

ON THE SEATTLE COURTHOUSE, DESIGN THE PROCESS UPS THE ANTE FOR FEDERAL PROJECTS

When we launched the project, our team considered the delivery track record of similar federal projects. We realized that most ended in claims and litigation. Right then all of us—the judiciary, the GSA, and the design consultants—determined that we were going to write a different story. To do that we designed the process by which we would all collaborate before designing the project. We built deliberate activities into our game plan that would bring us together as a team, challenge our thinking, and allow us to discover ideas together, such as our touring activities and the effort to speak a common language. We defined our roles and set performance expectations together. We crafted a framework for decision-making from start to finish in order to realize design excellence while delivering the entire project on time and on budget. Along the way we actively cultivated understanding and built a team culture of empathy between the court, the GSA, the design team, and the builders.

STEVE McCONNELL, PARTNER, NBBJ

MAP IT

Want to get where you're going? Draw a map.

Even in uncharted territory, mapping your route before you begin the journey ensures you'll get to your intended destination. You can always change direction along the way, but at least you'll have a framework to help you understand where you've been and where you're going. When you get there, you'll be able to find your way back again because you'll have a record of how enterprise need was met through design.

CATEGORY:
Delivery

GOAL:
Connecting design response to what's needed to move an enterprise forward.

ON SOUTHWEST WASHINGTON MEDICAL CENTER, MAP IT TARGETS THE NEED AND TRACKS THE DESIGN DECISIONS TO GET THERE

We did an immersive discovery phase and what became clear was that incremental improvements to the status quo wouldn't be enough for this hospital, given that it was facing a rapidly changing healthcare market and a very competitive landscape. So, we started by identifying specific organizational drivers and made them the first co-ordinates on a map that we used to keep our design journey on track, all the way from pre-design to post-occupancy. We flowed enterprise needs and the design decisions that came out of them into this framework, and it helped the team take what had started out as intangible goals and turn them into tangible results. With the map, we could readily distill ideas from a wide range of initial concepts into focused, specific objectives that would set the parameters for measuring performance once the project was complete.

RICHARD DALLAM, PARTNER, NBBJ

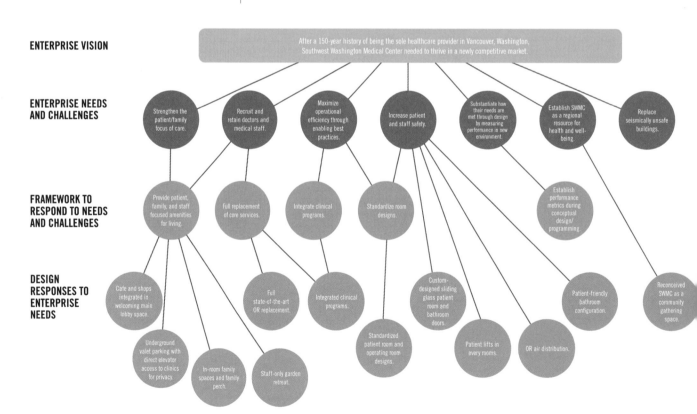

ENTERPRISE VISION

After a 150-year history of being the sole healthcare provider in Vancouver, Washington, Southwest Washington Medical Center needed to thrive in a newly competitive market.

ENTERPRISE NEEDS AND CHALLENGES

Strengthen the patient/family focus of care.

Recruit and retain doctors and medical staff.

Maximize operational efficiency through enabling best practices.

Increase patient and staff safety.

Substantiate how their needs are met through design by measuring performance in new environment.

Establish SWMC as a regional resource for health and well-being.

Replace seismically unsafe buildings.

FRAMEWORK TO RESPOND TO NEEDS AND CHALLENGES

Provide patient, family, and staff focused amenities for living.

Full replacement of core services.

Integrate clinical programs.

Standardize room designs.

Establish performance metrics during conceptual design/programming.

DESIGN RESPONSES TO ENTERPRISE NEEDS

Cafe and shops integrated in welcoming main lobby space.

Underground valet parking with direct elevator access to clinics for privacy.

In-room family spaces and family perch.

Full state-of-the-art OR replacement.

Integrated clinical programs.

Staff-only garden retreat.

Standardized patient room and operating room designs.

Custom-designed sliding glass patient room and bathroom doors.

Patient lifts in every rooms.

OR air distribution.

Patient-friendly bathroom configuration.

Reconceived SWMC as a community gathering space.

CHANGE DESIGN

DESIGNING FUTURES

Five NBBJ design teams share their insights as they work through design solutions for the next generation of Change Design projects. Informed by the experiences to date of the Change Design initiative and selected for their potential to transform a range of enterprise, including educational, healthcare, philanthropic, and residential, these conversations offer an inside look at NBBJ's work as it is unfolding and provide a window into the thinking that creates performance-based design. These "on the boards" projects are poised to become touchstones for testing and measuring the success of Change Design to come.

AT HOME IN THE WORLD

How does the Gates Foundation root itself in the place that nurtured it, while broadcasting its bold philanthropic mission to the global community it serves?

Guided by the belief that every life has equal value, the Bill & Melinda Gates Foundation works to help all people lead healthy, productive lives, in developing countries and in the United States. The foundation is outgrowing its office space, which is spread over multiple buildings in Seattle, and needs a new, long-term headquarters. It has acquired a site adjacent to the Seattle Center, an appropriate location for the organization to continue its outreach through regional and global programs. The design team discusses how the new campus can create an environment that serves as an effective workspace and embodies the foundation's mission and work.

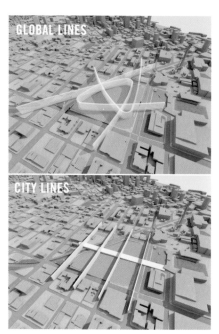

LINES OF INFLUENCE

The Pacific Northwest is home to the foundation's leaders and they chose to make their new headquarters in the urban core of Seattle. The work they do from here reaches to the most poverty-stricken areas of the globe. The client's descriptor is "local roots, global mission," and the new campus is a physical embodiment of that. The first two stories of the buildings are locked into the city grid with simple orthogonal forms. Above that level, the building forms reach out in different directions to the world beyond.

WORK PLACE LIVING ROOM

We worked with the foundation to develop a set of design precepts. They are used as guidelines and checklists, to make sure our work is embodying the foundation's mission and meeting its workplace needs. Three of the precepts involve the ideas of collaboration, community, and scale: spaces that promote interaction, convey common purpose, and appeal to all sizes of gatherings. The atrium meets those three precepts: it can be configured for an intimate, ad hoc get together or a formal address by a visiting dignitary.

THE CAMPUS HEART

The foundation's staff spends a significant amount of time traveling. When they are in Seattle it is important that they're able to share knowledge critical to their difficult mission. We've created a variety of work venues on an urban campus to provide the maximum opportunities for people to circulate, connect, and sit down together to discuss ideas and solutions.

GREEN ALL THE WAY TO THE TOP (TOP)

From the Space Needle, people will be able to look down on the campus and see that the lower portions of the campus and the garages have green roofs — together they will add up to the largest area of green roof in the northwest. There is a category in the project's design precepts for sustainability. These rooftops, planted with living organic material, are just one of the sustainable features on campus that speak to those precepts, from developing the site to enhance local ecosystems and maximize water conservation, to designing for well-being.

BOLD OUTREACH (MIDDLE)

One of the foundation's priorities is optimism. They take on difficult problems, such as hunger and disease, and are confident that they will be solved but perhaps not within the lifetime of the current staff. So it is critical that the workplace environment helps inspire optimism in staff. The campus design must also communicate this optimism to the local and global communities. The cantilevered buildings are a visual indicator of the foundation's boldness.

OPEN AIR FOYER (BOTTOM)

The entrance to the foundation is pulled away from the street and in toward the center of the campus. A landscaped plaza leads to the entry pavilion. The plaza provides a welcoming outdoor foyer for all the foundation's staff and visitors, as well as a new open space for the public.

CIVICS CLASS

How does Cleveland State University's College of Education and Human Services build a collaborative space for teachers and learners to connect with each other and the city they serve?

Cleveland is the poorest big city in the United States, according to the Census Bureau's American Community Survey, with nearly a third of the city's residents living in poverty. With its historical lifeline—manufacturing—eroding and with the global shift to knowledge-based economies, the city of Cleveland needs to provide its citizens with hope and education. Cleveland State University is a key player in meeting the challenge, since its College of Education and Human Services prepares educators devoted to social justice and urban needs. The college needs a new building that will foster a community of learning. NBBJ discusses how design can help decrease the distance—physical, intellectual and social—between teachers, learners, and citizens, and extend hope into the greater community of Cleveland.

GREETING THE STREET AND CITY

CSU's campus edge stretches along Euclid Avenue, a main arterial in Cleveland. The majority of buildings here are pulled away from the street and face inward onto the campus. We sited the building on the edge of the street as a new landmark to promote visibility and connectivity with the city. For commuters into the city it will signal the entrance to downtown and the revitalization of Cleveland.

LEARNERS

Through our research we discovered that most of the students at the college are elementary and secondary level teachers who take classes at night then go back out into the community the next morning, so the engagements they have in the building are applied quickly and positively in the city's neighborhoods.

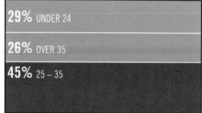

29% UNDER 24

26% OVER 35

45% 25 – 35

STUDENT AGE

25% MALE

75% FEMALE

STUDENT GENDER

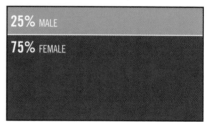

20% FULL TIME EMPLOYMENT

65% PART TIME EMPLOYMENT

15% NO EMPLOYMENT

UNDERGRADUATE EMPLOYMENT

65% FULL TIME EMPLOYMENT

20% PART TIME EMPLOYMENT

15% NO EMPLOYMENT

GRADUATE EMPLOYMENT

PAST, PRESENT AND FUTURE

The boundaries between Teacher (T) and Learner (L) are much more diffuse than they used to be. Rather than a traditional "knowledge transfer," learning is now more of a "knowledge network." The question this raised for the design team was, "How will the College of Education's new building help decrease the distance—intellectual, pedagogical, and social—between collaborators?"

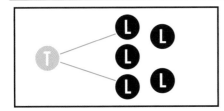

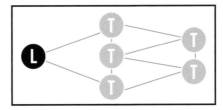

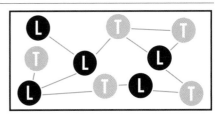

PAST: Knowledge Delivered. The traditional hierarchy of learning is knowledge as a one-way transfer from one teacher to a group of learners.

PRESENT: Knowledge Sharing. Multiple sources of knowledge and the proliferation of information through technology are shifting the learning dynamic to focus on the learner rather than the teacher.

FUTURE: Knowledge Network. Advances in technology will shift the boundaries between teacher and learner, allowing both to work together in networks of innovation-oriented learning.

PROGRAMMING THE SPACE

The traditional classroom is still an important educational environment. But we observed that learning was also happening before and after class—in seminar rooms, faculty offices, and even in circulation areas. We walked the college's leaders through a series of maps showing how learning zones could be integrated to break down disciplines and encourage collaborative learning. Our goal was to make the entire building a classroom that could grow and transform over time as people became more comfortable with new ways of learning

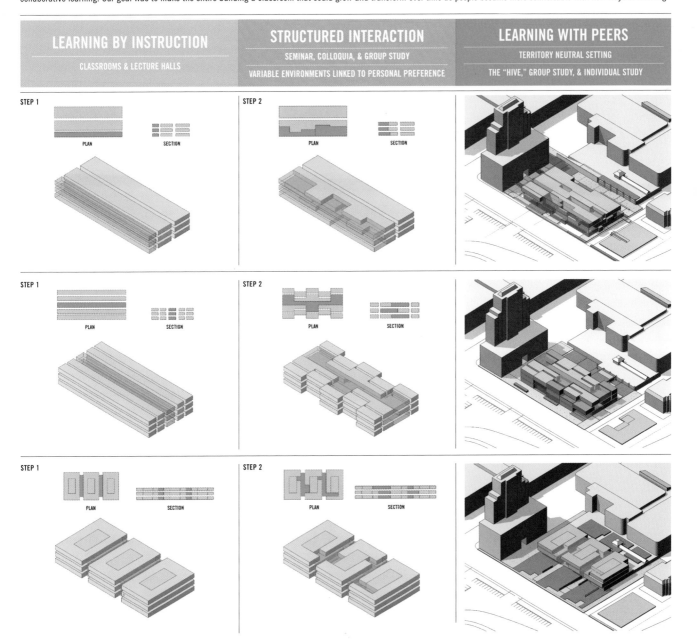

LEARNING BY INSTRUCTION	STRUCTURED INTERACTION	LEARNING WITH PEERS
CLASSROOMS & LECTURE HALLS	SEMINAR, COLLOQUIA, & GROUP STUDY	TERRITORY NEUTRAL SETTING
	VARIABLE ENVIRONMENTS LINKED TO PERSONAL PREFERENCE	THE "HIVE," GROUP STUDY, & INDIVIDUAL STUDY

STEP 1 · PLAN · SECTION

STEP 2 · PLAN · SECTION

THE FORUM (TOP)

The main public space, the forum, is the confluence of all the college's functions, and we wanted to make this clearly visible. We cut openings into a wall to provide views into adjacent classrooms. Only a glass wall separates the forum and the street-level computer lab which is accessible to students and, during certain times of the week, to the broader community.

LEARNING AS INTERFACE (BOTTOM)

So much learning today comes via interfaces: devices and systems that link and overlap. We catalogued them—from cell phones to smart boards—and the activities they allow, then visualized the outcomes in the space.

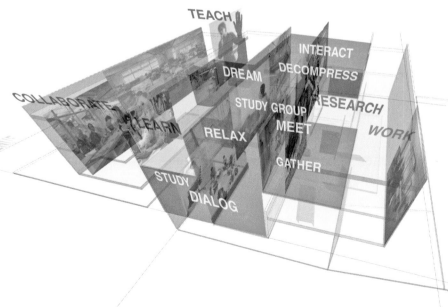

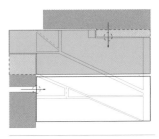

BUILDING ALONG EUCLID AVE.

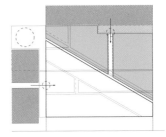

A CONNECTIVE GARDEN

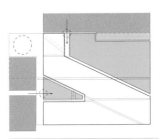

CARVED PLAZA SPACE

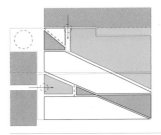

ACTIVE PUBLIC ZONES

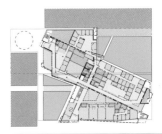

COMPOSITE SITE PLAN

TRANSPARENT AND CONNECTED

The new building aims to put education on display and connect what goes on there with everything else that's happening at CSU and the city at large. We used a lot of glass on the façade, so that those inside can see out, and those outside can see in. We oriented the building on a diagonal with plazas to the left and right. They'll be thoroughfares between the campus and Euclid Avenue.

URBAN FIT

How does Massachusetts General, one of America's oldest and most renowned hospitals, advance medical care, enable inevitable change, and support technical sophistication—all on a constrained urban site?

In 2011, Massachusetts General Hospital will be 200 years old. Over the past two centuries, this Boston landmark has built a solid reputation for providing the most advanced quality care, while amassing a complex variety of medical facilities in which to deliver that care. The hospital is marking its bicentennial with a new addition to its compact campus in downtown Boston. Dubbed the Building for the Third Century, or B3C, it must be an enduring structure that will meet MGH's needs, and serve and grow with the community for the next 100 years. As the NBBJ design team explains, B3C must also fit seamlessly into the existing campus and create for it a new center of excellence.

BREAKING CONSTRAINTS

The project brief specified a shift from double patient rooms to single patient rooms for the benefit of infection control, privacy, and greater patient/family-centered care. This doubles the floor plate, which increases the distance nurses have to travel from patient to patient, and further separates clinical collaborators who work in close proximity. Site constraints and the square floor plate of the patient tower made it challenging to provide everyone access to daylight. We sketched numerous options on how to minimize travel distances and maximize daylighting. The big "a-ha" was fracturing and shifting the floor plate to break apart the nursing pods and create a central circulation spine for wayfinding, natural light, and greater clinical connection.

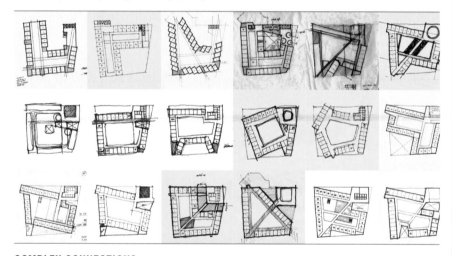

COMPLEX CONNECTIONS

The B3C provides and relies on access and connections to the existing campus. These connections are necessary for material flow (the loading dock in B3C will supply the entire campus), for patient transport to services elsewhere on campus, and for a seamless Emergency Department addition.

SERVING CONSTITUENCIES

The patient tower has to serve three major constituencies. These diagrams helped us visualize how the patient floors will serve each of these users equitably. The public access zones appear in green, the patient rooms in blue, and the working spaces for nurses and clinical support staff in orange.

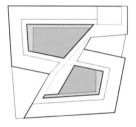

PATIENT ROOMS

STAFF WORK AREAS

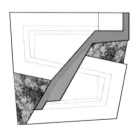

PUBLIC ACCESS

PATIENT FLOOR COMPOSITE

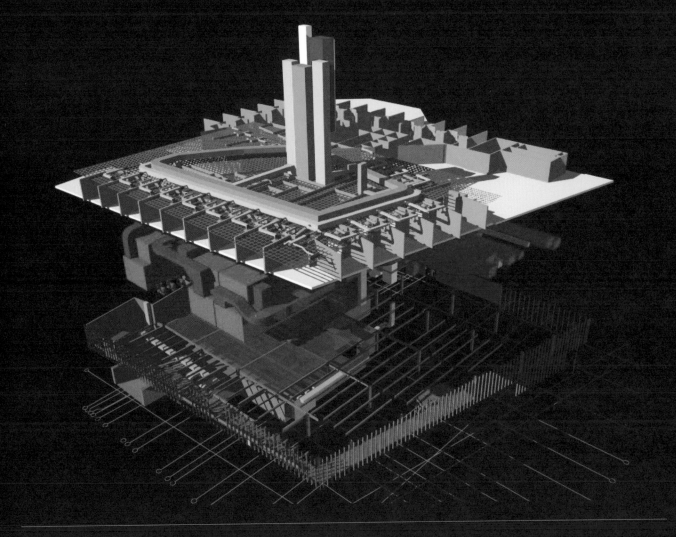

MANAGING COMPLEXITY

The B3C is an incredibly complex building. It needs to connect to five other existing buildings on the campus; link, internally, a number of different programmatic elements; and it also needs to be flexible to accommodate future change. We used state-of-the-art computer technologies, called Building Information Modeling, or BIM, to work with our subconsultants to fit all the pieces together. Using BIM we created a working 3D model where each member of the design team was able to layer in trade-specific details as the design progressed. We used this model to develop every element of the building, from planning intent, structural, mechanical and electrical systems to its interiors. Built-in "collision detection" systems allowed us to identify problems early in the design process and find solutions before the start of construction. BIM has also been a great communication tool for sharing ideas with the building's users and obtaining city approvals. Our construction manager has used the model to demonstrate how the building is being phased to avoid on-site complications.

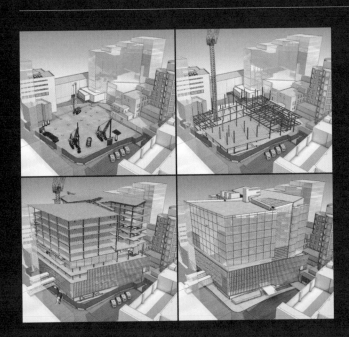

INSIDE INTELLIGENCE

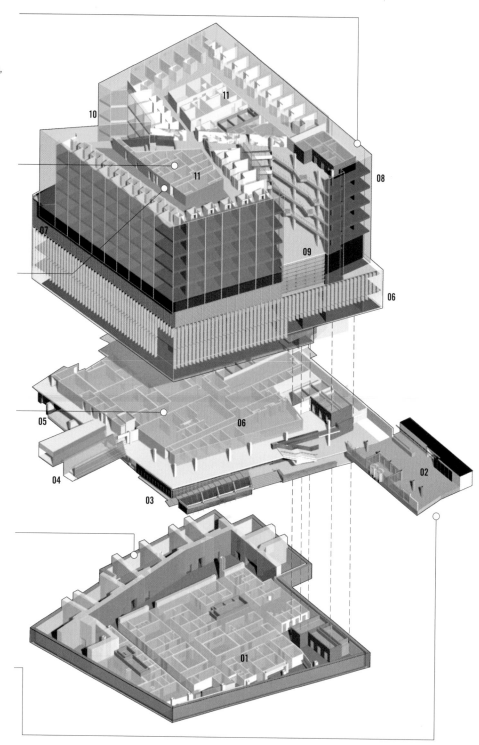

Elevator cores are carefully located to avoid interference with the Radiation Oncology vaults, ambulance ramp and parking, loading dock, and public connector. The building has 11 elevators and lifts for transporting visitors to patient floors, providing privacy for patient travel, and behind-the-scenes delivery for material flow.

To preserve quiet and calm, nurse support activities are tucked into interior corridors so patients won't hear doors banging, or nurses working, or see clutter in the main corridor.

Corridors in the nursing unit are wider than normal and are equipped with computer stations across from patient rooms to allow for teaching and informal communication among clinicians without disturbing corridor traffic, or violating patient privacy.

Patient preparation and instrument set-up occur in separate rooms adjacent to the OR, while the OR is being cleaned. This reduces the down time between operations, improving flow and the number of cases performed per day.

The eight linear accelerator vaults in the Radiation Oncology department have slightly different geometries to fit the irregular building perimeter. Different circulation paths for newly diagnosed patients are provided to avoid stressful encounters during initial visits.

A bridge over the existing lobby provides ease of flow for surgical patients and their families between buildings, as well as a clear route for the new sterile processing department in B3C, which supports the entire campus.

01 Radiation Oncology department (basement C & D)
02 Main (existing) entrance lobby and connector to MGH campus
03 Emergency Department addition (level 1)
04 Bridge to Yawkey building—ambulatory center (level 2)
05 Ambulance entry ramp
06 Procedure floors (levels 2-4)

07 Mechanical floor (level 5)
08 Patient tower (levels 6-10)
09 Interior garden atrium
10 Exterior garden
11 Nurse and clinical staff work areas

Not shown: Sterile Processing (Basement B), Materials Management/Loading Dock (Basement A)

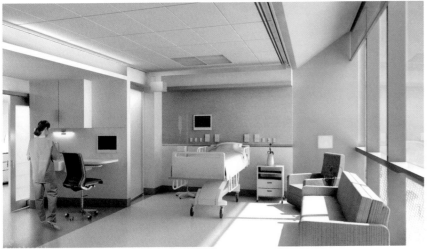

LETTING THE LIGHT IN (TOP)

A connection to the outdoors and natural light is known to speed up the healing process. Naturally lit spaces also have diagnostic benefits for patients and staff, as well as operational and sustainable benefits by decreasing reliance on electrical energy. We designed all the patient rooms to have full-height windows, uninterrupted views, and access to daylight. By fracturing the patient floor plan with a central circulation spine, nurses' stations at the core of the patient tower can receive ample amounts of natural light. We also designed a five-story atrium as an interior garden oasis for patients, visitors, and staff. The atrium allows daylighting to reach patient rooms located on the building's inner core and provides patients and families with views onto the interior garden, and beyond the atrium to the outdoors.

ENHANCING SATISFACTION (BOTTOM)

The more time spent caring for a patient, whether by a nurse or the patient's family, increases the levels of satisfaction for everyone involved. The patient room is designed to enhance these critical connections. We designed distinct areas for clinical staff, the patient, and visiting family, that allow space for each to carry out their duties or rest, while maintaining a constant visual connection to each other.

CLIMATE CHANGE

How can a high-rise introduce strategies for living in a hot, humid climate while also providing its residents with practices for a more sustainable lifestyle?

City Developments Limited (CDL), a leading residential developer in Singapore, has built more than 22,000 homes, many in the city's upper-level real estate market. Cities in tropical climates have the density to be inherently sustainable and, for the past two decades, CDL has been promoting green living by introducing sustainable features in their residences. CDL's two 24-story towers on Grange Road are aimed at young families for whom luxury and wellness are twin priorities. The challenge for NBBJ's design team, as they narrate here, is to target building performance to meet Singapore Building & Construction Authority's Green Mark rating and offer buyers a home that meets their goals for a well appointed, sustainable lifestyle.

SUN SCREEN

The Building & Construction Authority's stringent requirements for a building envelope's thermal performance are necessary because of Singapore's climate. We studied the heat gain across both towers' façades to determine which areas needed the most shading. Based on these studies we designed a building envelope system that uses fritted glass to insulate and shade areas of intense sun exposure and incorporated balconies into the building's design to provide additional areas of shading in the units.

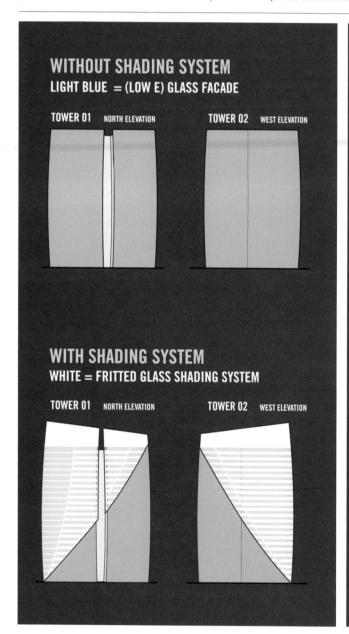

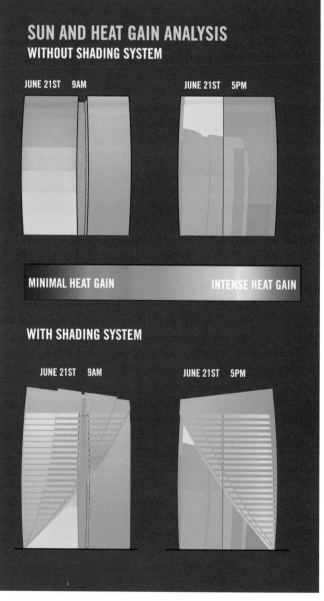

TURNING DOWN THE AC

Singapore's climate makes it among the world's highest per capita users of air conditioning. However, in the shade and in the evenings it's pleasant to be outdoors. The project is pursuing a Green Mark Platinum rating (equivalent to LEED Gold), so we're incorporating passive low-energy strategies that will make it not only possible but also attractive to turn the air conditioning down, or off entirely. All units have open-air extensions to the living rooms to encourage residents to open up their units when cooler.

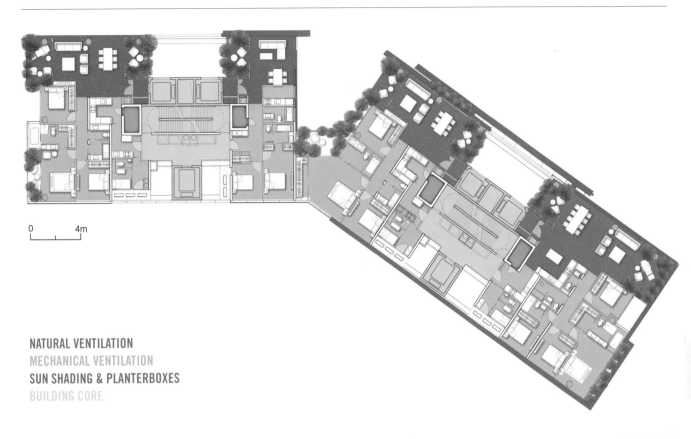

0   4m

NATURAL VENTILATION
MECHANICAL VENTILATION
SUN SHADING & PLANTERBOXES
BUILDING CORE

INDOOR COMFORT

In addition to the fritted glass on the buildings' exterior, all bedrooms have operable windows and are equipped with motorized solar screens that can be manually controlled or set to automatically lower during certain times of the day. This gives residents some individual control over sun-shading and allows them to regulate the indoor temperature of their apartments without having to resort to air conditioning all the time.

LET IT RAIN

Singapore gets a tremendous amount of rainfall, but doesn't have its own freshwater source. The bend in the building exposes the balcony roofs: that increases the surface available to capture rainwater. Because it's collected by the balconies and mullions on the curved face before it hits the ground, this harvested rainwater can be used for non-potable uses, such as irrigating the grounds, without being treated first.

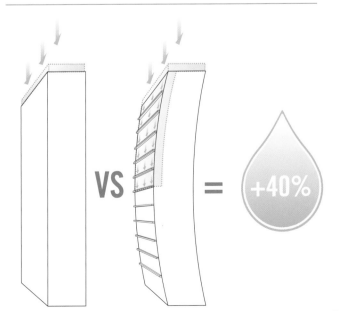

VS = +40%

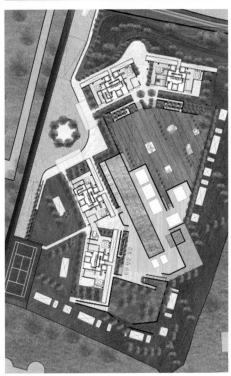

THE VERTICAL GARDEN

The Grange Road area has many mature trees, and we'll be doing extensive landscaping on site. There will be very little hard surface paving, since parking is underground. The buildings will be forms in a lush landscape. But for people living in a highrise to feel connected to nature, they need more than green grounds. We developed the concept of a vertical garden to draw the landscape upward and tie each unit to the earth. As residents travel up in the windowed elevator, they'll see vegetation below, on the balconies of each floor, and inside the entrance to their own home.

THE EXPERIENCE EQUATION

How does health provider Kaiser Permanente connect the dots between what the organization believes and says, and what its members see and experience?

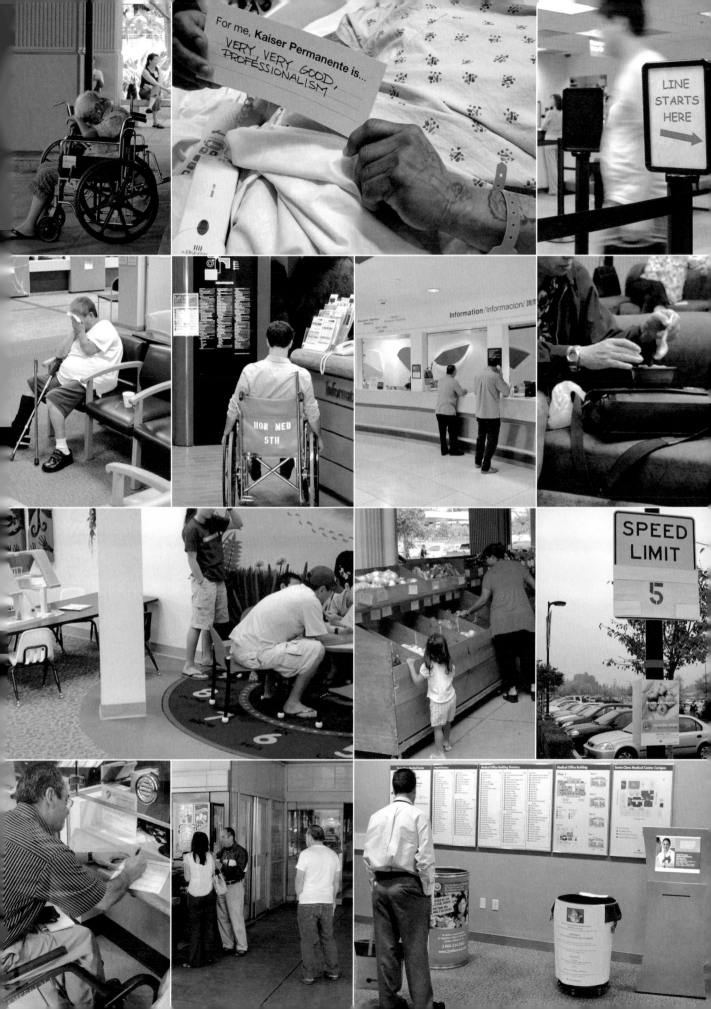

Kaiser Permanente has identified an opportunity to define itself in the context of "total health." Rather than looking to a traditional healthcare, or "sick care" model, Kaiser Permanente's integrated delivery model and philosophy of preventive care focuses on optimizing the balance of mind, body, and spirit. Kaiser Permanente intends to leverage their built environment to communicate to the organization's members an understanding of their needs, emotions, aspirations for the future, and outlook on health. The NBBJ design team's challenge was to develop an understanding of how Kaiser Permanente's facilities could speak the voice of the brand and deliver on the promise of an environment that supports "total health."

THE KAISER PERMANENTE EXPERIENCE EQUATION

Our human-centered process for understanding people's needs and emotions and for exploring future opportunities with them can be expressed as an equation: CONTEXT (the entire set of circumstances that come to bear on any given situation) + EMOTIONS (the state of mind one is in as a result of their circumstance) + JOURNEY (the path people travel through space and time) + TOUCH POINTS (the events, services, interactions, and artifacts people encounter along their journey) = THEIR EXPERIENCE.

1 CLIENT	**8** REGIONS	**18** HOSPITALS	**26** MOB'S AND CLINICS	**19** WEEKS
6 RESEARCH METHODS	**11** WORKSHOPS	**9** NBBJ TEAM MEMBERS	**7** CLIENT TEAM MEMBERS	**121** PATIENTS
=	**180** ENVIRONMENTAL, OPERATIONAL AND STRATEGIC OPPORTUNITIES	**5** PRINCIPLES TO IMPROVE EXPERIENCE	**10** CONCEPTS TO DIRECT DESIGN EFFORTS	**21** CRITICAL EXPERIENCE ZONES IN A TYPICAL HEALTHCARE JOURNEY

FROM DISCOVERY TO DELIVERY

To align environment with experience, we use a number of tools that take us from discovery, to translation, and finally to delivery. On the following pages we look at how we are using those tools on the Kaiser Permanente project.

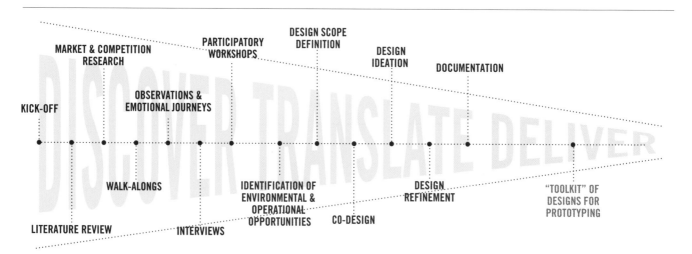

KICK-OFF · MARKET & COMPETITION RESEARCH · OBSERVATIONS & EMOTIONAL JOURNEYS · PARTICIPATORY WORKSHOPS · DESIGN SCOPE DEFINITION · DESIGN IDEATION · DOCUMENTATION

LITERATURE REVIEW · WALK-ALONGS · INTERVIEWS · IDENTIFICATION OF ENVIRONMENTAL & OPERATIONAL OPPORTUNITIES · CO-DESIGN · DESIGN REFINEMENT · "TOOLKIT" OF DESIGNS FOR PROTOTYPING

DISCOVER TRANSLATE DELIVER

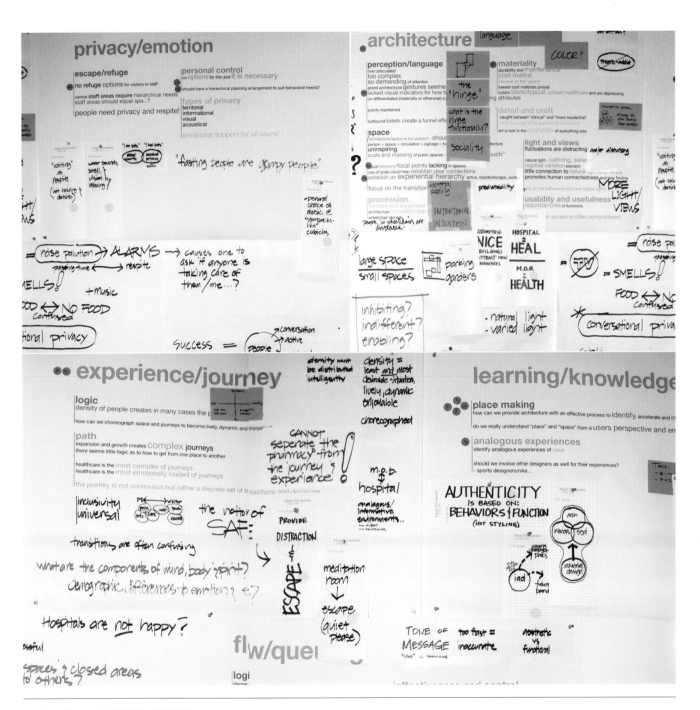

RESEARCH TO BUSINESS IMPACT

To visualize the environmental, operational, and strategic opportunities and prioritize design efforts, we mapped all the ideas we had gathered and generated onto targets and voted on the most critical items. This activity has defined our scope of work and highlighted the fundamental dependence betweens all parts of the healthcare system—environment, operations, behavior, and culture. The map helped us make the point that without synergy across the organization, the environmental design by itself is in jeopardy of failure.

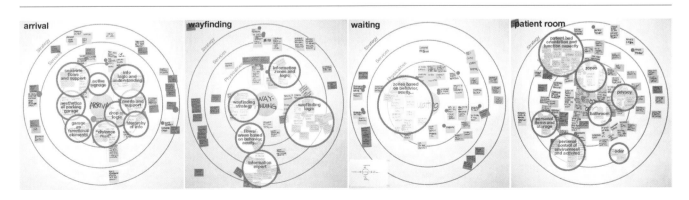

EXPLORE THE EXPERIENCE

Our process on the Kaiser Permanente project began with a review of the existing brand literature and research on the competition. The next step was to conduct "walk-alongs"— quick, broad explorations of many facilities to understand the context of Kaiser Permanente. In our research and discovery phase on Kaiser Permanente we used a number of other tools, including: Observation, an immersive and strategic exploration of key facilities to explore complex circumstances in depth; interviews, which we define as interactive conversations with people to understand their thoughts and feelings during their visit; emotional journeys, in which we take a journey specific to a health condition in order to explore specific needs and emotions; and participatory workshops, which are creative exercises to empower people to think about opportunities for the future.

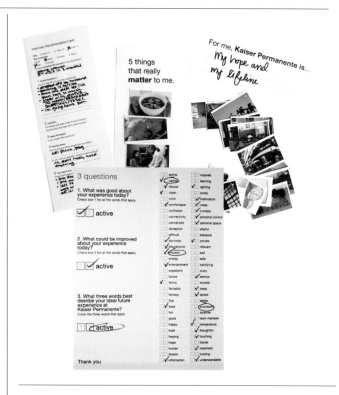

OBSERVATIONS

INTERVIEWS

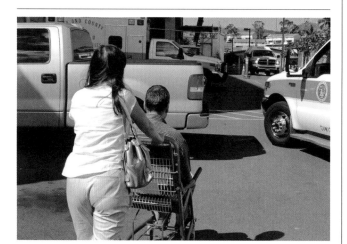

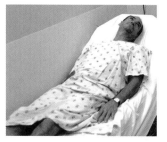

WALK A MILE IN THEIR SHOES

PARTICIPATORY WORKSHOPS

MAPPING THE EXPERIENCE

We discovered that healthcare experiences differ drastically depending on circumstance—patient/visitor, planned/un-planned, hospital stay/doctor's visit. Despite those differences, design seems to respond uniformly, failing to support people in a way that is relevant to their specific circumstance. We mapped these journeys, and used the maps to help guide the environmental impact of our work.

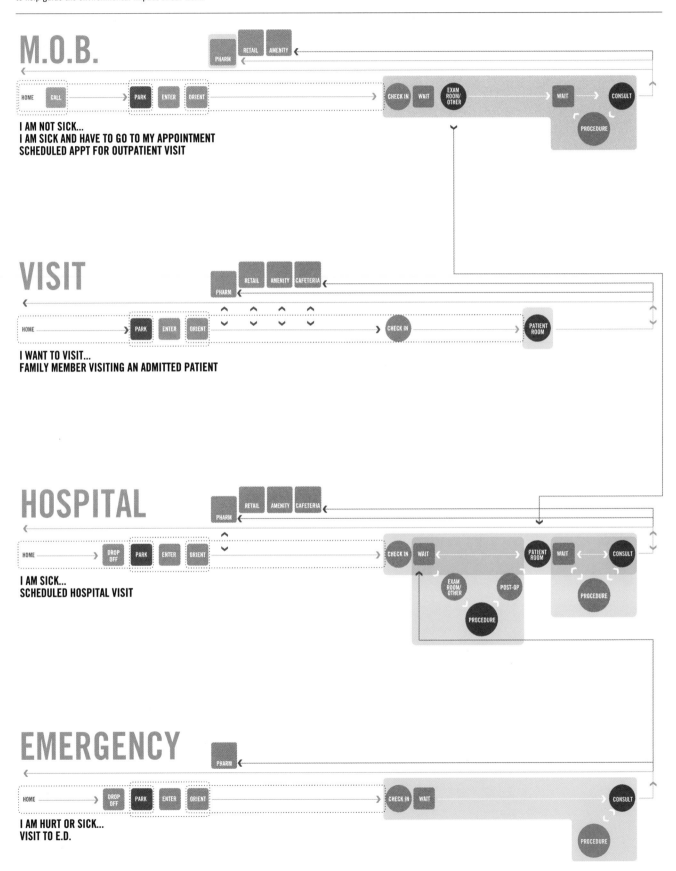

M.O.B.

I AM NOT SICK...
I AM SICK AND HAVE TO GO TO MY APPOINTMENT
SCHEDULED APPT FOR OUTPATIENT VISIT

VISIT

I WANT TO VISIT...
FAMILY MEMBER VISITING AN ADMITTED PATIENT

HOSPITAL

I AM SICK...
SCHEDULED HOSPITAL VISIT

EMERGENCY

I AM HURT OR SICK...
VISIT TO E.D.

21 CRITICAL EXPERIENCES

Our research helped us identify "21 Critical Experiences," the key moments along a healthcare journey from a patient's point of view. Our design work addressing these experiences is currently being prototyped and tested for further development.

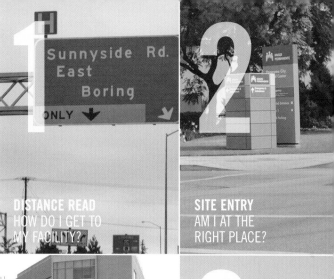

1

DISTANCE READ
HOW DO I GET TO
MY FACILITY?

2

SITE ENTRY
AM I AT THE
RIGHT PLACE?

6

**GETTING TO THE
FACILITY** WHERE AM I
GOING AND HOW
DO I GET THERE?

7

EXTERIOR ENTRANCE
WHICH FACILITY SHOULD
I GO TO?

8

INTERIOR ENTRANCE
WHERE IS THE
INFORMATION DESK?

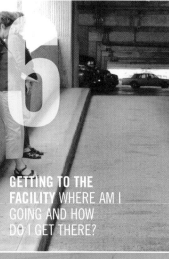

12

STAFF SPACES
WHERE CAN I TAKE
A BREAK?

13

14

OUTDOOR SPACES
WHERE CAN I
ESCAPE AND RELAX?

15

CAFE
WHERE CAN I GRAB A
BITE TO EAT AND CHAT?

17

FARMERS MARKET
DO I NEED ANYTHING ELSE
WHILE I AM HERE?

WAITING
WHERE CAN I GO
PLAY MOM?

18

CONSULT
WHAT IS GOING ON
WITH ME?

3
SITE ORIENTATION
WHICH WAY DO
I GO NOW?

4
PARKING
WHERE IS AN
EMPTY SPOT?

5
DROP OFF / PICK UP
WHERE CAN I MEET YOU
AFTER I PARK?

9
formation/Informacion/詢問處

CHECK-IN
WHO CAN HELP
ME FIND MY DOCTOR?

10
CORRIDORS
HOW FAR IS IT?

11

**ELEVATORS
AND STAIRWELLS**
TO WHAT FLOOR DO
I NEED TO GO?

16

RETAIL
WHERE CAN I GET SOME
FLOWERS FOR MY WIFE?

19

GUEST ROOM
WHO WILL CARE
FOR ME?

20
BATHROOMS
WHERE CAN
I FRESHEN UP?

21

PROVIDER OFFICES
WHERE CAN I ADDRESS
THIS IN PRIVATE?

ACKNOWLEDGEMENTS

CHANGE CONVERSATIONS
(IN ORDER OF APPEARANCE)

Jon Fredrik Baksaas, President / CEO, Telenor; Susan Doria, Former Senior Vice President, Strategic Development Banner Health; Ada Healey, Vice President of Vulcan Real Estate; Lyle Bicknell, Senior Urban Designer, City of Seattle Department of Planning and Development; Carolyn Corvi, Former Vice President/General Manager, Airplane Production, Boeing Commercial Airplanes, The Boeing Company; John Cooper, Director of Resources, Wellcome Trust Sanger Institute; Allan Bradley, Director, Wellcome Trust Sanger Institute; Phil Butcher, Head of Information Technology, Wellcome Trust Sanger Institute; Jim Reed, Former Director of Fiscal Policy, Washington State Higher Education Coordinating Board; Bruce Rifkin, District Court Executive, United States District Court for the Western District of Washington; John C. Coughenour, Chief United States District Judge, Western District of Washington; Joseph Kortum, President and CEO, Southwest Washington Medical Center; Renate M. Atkins, Chief Operating Officer, Southwest Washington Medical Center; Larry Smarr, Director, California Institute for Telecommunications and Information Technology (Calit2).

We would also like to thank Dag Melgaard, Telenor; Jeff Nelson, Banner Estrella; Robin McBride and Craig Martin, The Boeing Company; Coke Putnam, HECB; and Stephanie Sides and Doug Ramsey, Calit2; Jennifer Bragg, The Fearey Group; Connie Chilcote and Donna Maple, Southwest Washington Medical Center.

The Telenor project covered in this section was designed as a joint venture between NBBJ-HUS-PKA. Banner Estrella and Banner Gateway were designed by NBBJ in partnership with Phoenix-based Orcutt Winslow Partnership.

CHANGE DESIGN ESSAYS
(IN ORDER OF APPEARANCE)

Daniel Pink, Author; Bruce Mau, Author and Founder, Bruce Mau Design; Jeanne Liedtka, Professor of Business Administration, University of Virginia, Darden Graduate School of Business; Alexi Marmot, Author and Founder, Alexi Marmot Associates; Richard Swett, Author and Senior Fellow, Design Futures Council; Roger Martin, Dean of Rotman School of Management, University of Toronto; Astrid Pujari, MD, MNIMH and Founder of the Pujari Center.

CHANGE DESIGN TOOLS

Many staff members at NBBJ helped in capturing and characterizing the Change Tools: Cam Allen, William Bain, Friedrich Böhm, Blaine Brownell, Christian Carlson, Anne Cunningham, Scott Dunlap, Jay Halleran, Liz Jacks, Bill Johnson, Jim Jonassen, Michael Kreis, Brad Leathley, Eric Levine, Charles Martin, Steve McConnell, AJ Montero, Bruce Nepp, Bill Nichols, JinAh Park, Fred Powell, Peter Pran, Martin Regge, Brent Rogers, Kristina Ryhn, Liz Sanders, Bill Sanford, George Simons, Jacob Simons, Lynne Shira, Rysia Suchecka, James Tully, Vince Vergel de Dios, Lori Walker, Jonathan Ward, and Alan Young.

CHANGE DESIGN FUTURES
(IN ORDER OF APPEARANCE)

Bill & Melinda Gates Foundation; Dr. Richard Hurwitz, Associate Dean, CoEHS; Dr. James A. McLoughlin, Dean, CoEHS; and Edward Schmittgen, Director of Capital Planning & University Architect, Cleveland State University; David J. Hanitchak, Director of Planning & Construction at Partners Healthcare; Chia Ngiang Hong, Group General Manager, City Developments Limited; Brenda Lee, Senior Manager, Head of Corporate Communications, City Developments Limited, Wong Chung Jeu, Senior Manager of Residential Projects, City Developments Limited; and Eddie Wong, General Manager (Projects), City Developments Limited; Debbie Cantu, Vice President, Brand Marketing and Advertising at Kaiser Permanente.

Many staff members at NBBJ helped in telling the Change Design Futures stories: At Home in the World: Christian Carlson, Anne Cunningham, Kelly Griffin, John Hendry, Steve McConnell, Hau Vong; Civics Class: Brad Leathley, AJ Montero, Jason Richardson, Andy Snyder; Urban Fit: Craig Brimley, Sarah Markowitz, Joan Saba, Jay Siebenmorgen, Christine Vandover; Climate Change: Hannah Ilten, Tim Johnson, Will Robertson; The Experience Equation: Eric Levine, George Simons, Jacob Simons.

CHANGE DESIGN SECOND EDITION EDITORIAL TEAM

IR&Co.: Ian Rapsey.

StudioLAB: Cathy Jonasson.

Sparkler Communications: Angelica Fox.

NBBJ: Richard Dallam, Timothy Johnson, Steve McConnell, Scott Wyatt; Editorial: Janet Chung, Helen Dimoff, Andrea Larsen.

Special thanks for their work on the first edition and for their insights, advice, and expertise:

Bruce Mau Design: Bruce Mau, Jim Shedden, Kevin Sugden, and Michael Waldin.

NBBJ: Sean Airhart, Bonnie Duncan, Tim Juchter, Dena Pereira, Sonya Poland and Margo Sepanski.

PHOTOGRAPHY AND ILLUSTRATION

Sean Airhart, Tom Arban, Benjamin Benschneider, Craig Brookes, Gudmundur Brynjarsson, Peter Cook, Crystal Computer Graphics Ltd, Bruce Damonte, Alan Decker/NY Times, Scott Dunlap, John Durant, Jeff Goldberg / Esto, Tim Griffith, Gustafson Guthrie Nichol Ltd, Damian Heinisch, Robert Hood, James F. Housel, Timothy Hursley, Steve Keating, Andrea Jeanne Larsen, Ronghui Li, John Linden, Michelle Litvin, IoMedia, Steve McConnell, Matt Milios, Robert Murray, Frank Ooms, Pixelcraft, Inc., Don Powell / Wellcome images, Christian Richters, Matthew Roharik, Brian Smale, Matt Schoolfield, Kim Selby, George Simons, Jacob Simons, Sherry Snow, Timothy Soar, Lara Swimmer, Turner Construction, D. Visser, George White, and Scott Wyatt.

Thank you to Jim Cramer of Östberg Press and David Li, Becky Dalmasi, and Carol Isaacson, Oceanic Graphic Printing (USA), Inc.

IF WE COULD LET WORKING GROUPS MEET
EACH OTHER IN A MORE EASY PHYSICAL
ATMOSPHERE, IT WOULD GENERATE NEW
IDEAS, REDUCE TIME TO MARKET, AND KEEP
PACE WITH MARKET DEVELOPMENTS.

JON FREDRIK BAKSAAS

CREATIVE PEOPLE WORKING TOGETHER WILL GENERATE GOOD IDEAS. IT'S A MATTER OF BUILDING AN ENVIRONMENT THAT FACILITATES THAT.

JOHN COOPER

I'VE HEARD MANY PEOPLE SAY, "IT'S AMAZING. OUR PRODUCTIVITY'S INCREASED SINCE WE'VE MOVED IN." CONSIDERING ALL THE UPSET CAUSED BY MOVING INTO A NEW BUILDING, IT'S QUITE INTERESTING THAT PEOPLE ARE ALREADY FEELING A POSITIVE IMPACT.

PHIL BUTCHER

WE BENCHMARK OURSELVES AGAINST OTHER PEER ORGANIZATIONS AROUND THE COUNTRY, AND BANNER ESTRELLA HOSPITAL IS HITTING THE 99TH PERCENTILE IN PATIENT SATISFACTION. PEOPLE HAVE NEW TOOLS TO PROVIDE BETTER CARE.

SUSAN DORIA

JUDGES CAME FROM NEW AND OLD
COURTHOUSES ALL OVER THE COUNTRY AND
WE TOURED THEM THROUGH THE BUILDING.
THEY SAID "MY GOD, THAT MAKES SENSE.
WHAT A FUNCTIONAL PLACE."

BRUCE RIFKIN

WHEN YOU THINK ABOUT PROGRESSIVE BUILDINGS, BUILDINGS THAT DON'T USE AS MUCH ENERGY, BUILDINGS THAT REALLY SUPPORT EMPLOYEE PRODUCTIVITY, YOU'VE GOT TO THINK A BIT OUT OF THE BOX.

ADA HEALEY

WHEN OUR BUILDING STARTED COMING
OUT OF THE GROUND AND PEOPLE COULD SEE
WHAT WAS GOING TO HAPPEN, IT WAS AMAZING.
WE RAISED $53 MILLION, WHICH FOR OUR
COMMUNITY WAS UNPRECEDENTED.

JOSEPH KORTUM

YOU CAN MAKE THE PHYSICAL
CHANGE BUT PROGRESS COMES FROM
PEOPLE INTERNALIZING IT AND THEN
CULTURALLY CHANGING THEIR BEHAVIOR
TO COMPLEMENT IT.

CAROLYN CORVI

THE DESIGN OF THE BUILDING ITSELF WAS
THE MOST IMPORTANT FORMATIVE ASPECT OF
CREATING OUR CULTURAL DNA.

LARRY SMARR